Waltraud Kokot (Ed.)

Living and Working in Sofia

l i n e s

Beiträge zur Stadtforschung
aus dem Institut für Ethnologie
der Universität Hamburg

herausgegeben von

Waltraud Kokot

Band 7

LIT

Living and Working in Sofia

Ethnographies of agency, social relations and livelihood strategies in the capital of Bulgaria

edited by

Waltraud Kokot

LIT

Cover Image: Kasper de Jong

Bibliographic information published by the Deutsche Nationalbibliothek
The Deutsche Nationalbibliothek lists this publication in the Deutsche Nationalbibliografie; detailed bibliographic data are available in the Internet at http://dnb.d-nb.de.

ISBN 978-3-643-90220-7

A catalogue record for this book is available from the British Library

Klosbachstr. 107
CH-8032 Zürich
Tel. +41 (0) 44-251 75 05
Fax +41 (0) 44-251 75 06
e-Mail: zuerich@lit-verlag.ch
http://www.lit-verlag.ch

LIT VERLAG Dr. W. Hopf
Berlin 2012
Fresnostr. 2
D-48159 Münster
Tel. +49 (0) 2 51-620 320
Fax +49 (0) 2 51-23 19 72
e-Mail: lit@lit-verlag.de
http://www.lit-verlag.de

Distribution:
In Germany: LIT Verlag Fresnostr. 2, D-48159 Münster
Tel. +49 (0) 2 51-620 32 22, Fax +49 (0) 2 51-922 60 99, e-mail: vertrieb@lit-verlag.de

In Austria: Medienlogistik Pichler-ÖBZ, e-mail: mlo@medien-logistik.at

In Switzerland: B + M Buch- und Medienvertrieb, e-mail: order@buch-medien.ch

In the UK: Global Book Marketing, e-mail: mo@centralbooks.com

Acknowledgements

This book has been made possible by the help and co-operation of a wide range of individuals and institutions. At the University of Hamburg, ethnographic fieldwork has been a core element of the course of studies in Social Anthropology for many years and will hopefully remain so also in the future. An important prerequisite for our fieldwork excursions has been the regular funding by the School of Humanities, Department of Cultural History and Contemporary Culture.

Friends and colleagues in Sofia have provided invaluable expert knowledge, local know-how and institutional support. Prof. Dr. Milena Benovska-Sabkova has played a key role in this project from the very beginning. She contributed significantly to the preparation of our fieldwork through guest lectures and seminars in Hamburg, by suggesting relevant literature and by offering practical support via e-mail. In Sofia, she brought together a group of graduate students and colleagues for a weekly joint seminar on fieldwork practice and research design. Besides sharing their own research interests, in these meetings Dr. Vihra Barova, Dr. Ana Luleva, Ivaylo Markov, Elena Petkova and Yana Yancheva gave us the opportunity to discuss and exchange our impressions and results from the field. They offered valuable contacts, information and constructive critique, both as ethnologists and as local experts. In particular, our special thanks go to Dr. Vihra Barova, who devoted a great deal of her time and energy to our project and shared important nodes of her social network with us.

Due to the generous hospitality offered by Dr. Michael Tachev, chief executive officer of St. Cyril and Methodius International Foundation, our meetings took place in the Foundation´s seminar rooms located in a central area of Sofia. By providing the rooms and infrastructure for our weekly sessions, the Foundation has contributed greatly to our project´s success. In particular, we also wish to thank Ms. Lilyana Nikolova, who helped our project both by organizational support and by much-needed advice on practical matters.

Most participants of this project did not have any prior knowledge of the Bulgarian language before joining the research group. Eleonora Wewer has taken on a double role in this project, both as a participant and as an experienced language teacher of her native Bulgarian. Thanks to her enthusiasm and relentlessness,all participants managed in little more than one year to learn enough Bulgarian to handle everyday situations, although most interviews eventually were conducted in English, German or Russian.

In many editorial sessions, Mascha Kern und Ivan Raduychev have helped preparing the texts for publication. In particular, Mascha´s work has been invaluable, as she also carried the burden of formatting the whole text and of adapting the layout. Finally, our thanks go to Dr. Rosemarie Oesselmann for proofreading the manuscript.

Last but most importantly, ethnographic fieldwork always depends on the people who are able and willing to devote their time and share their knowledge with the ethnographers. As the individual projects described in this book address very different topics, the persons who answered our questions and allowed us to observe their activities during our fieldwork in Sofia represent different generations and a variety of professions, institutions and ethnic or religious affiliations. Except for the few who explicitly wished their real names to be published, all others are referred to by pseudonyms in order to protect their privacy.

One of these people was Štěpán Helešic, who not only shared his knowledge, but also became a close friend to some of us. Shortly after our fieldwork, he died in a tragic accident. This book is dedicated to his memory.

Hamburg, March 2012

Contents

Map of central Sofia

Sofia Inner City (Source: http://mappery.com/Central-Sofia-Tourist-Map [retrieved 1.10.2011])

About the authors

Sinikka Harms, 26, studies Social Anthropology and History at Hamburg University. While spending one year of studies in Seville, Spain, she discovered art as a medium of expressing herself. For this reason, she focused on this topic also in her fieldwork in Sofia. Interested in the anthropology of art, she plans to write her Master's thesis in this field as well.

Mira Carla Höpfner was born in 1987 in Heidelberg, Germany. She is currently pursuing her major in Social Anthropology as well as minors in Political Science and Sociology at the University of Hamburg. Her interest in Anthropology was sparked by several years of living abroad in Indonesia, Libya, and Canada. Her passion for environmental issues motivated her to focus her field studies on environmental, non-governmental organizations (NGOs) in Bulgaria, as civil society continues to develop and grow there.

Mascha Kern studies Social Anthropology, Political Science and French at the University of Hamburg. Born 1987 in Kazakhstan, her Russian roots influenced the choice of her research topic, the resources of Russian-speaking migrants. Her interest in the anthropology of dance arose from her personal experience as a dancer (ballet, modern dance). Currently, she is planning field research for her Master's thesis on modern dance as an expressive cultural form in Sofia.

Renate Kleinknecht studies Social Anthropology and Art History at Hamburg University. Based on her experience with her own small trade enterprise, she focused her fieldwork in Sofia on research in small firms, especially small cafés.

Waltraud Kokot is professor of Social Anthropology at the University of Hamburg. Major topics of her research include urban anthropology and diaspora studies. Her regional interests focus on South-Eastern Europe, mainly on Greece (Thessaloniki) and Bulgaria (Sofia).

Katharina Kunze, born in 1982, worked as a copywriter before she turned to Social Anthropology, Gender Studies and Philosophy. She did three field studies in Israel, Germany, and Bulgaria - including *Animus Association Foundation* - in order to compare women's NGOs, their aims, strategies, working procedures and success. The results of this project will also be the theme of her Master's thesis.

Ivan Raduychev, born in 1981 in Pomorie, Bulgaria, has been living in Germany since 2000. He studies Social Anthropology and Psychology at the University of Hamburg and practices Vipassana Meditation since 2005. Ivan was involved in establishing the Bulgarian Vipassana Organisation in 2008, hence his interest in meditation and yoga also as topics of research.

Eleonora Wewer, 40, studied Literature and Culture at the University of Sofia, and European and Social Anthropology at the University of Hamburg. Her professional experience includes cross-cultural awareness trainings with a focus on Eastern Europe, as well as teaching Bulgarian as a foreign language. She is co-founder of *Postkartell Institute for Applied Cultural Studies* (www.postkartell.org).

Introduction: Ethnographic research in Sofia

Waltraud Kokot

"*Of all European capitals, Sofia has always remained the least known, the least familiar…*"

With these words, Philip Ward (1993: ii) introduced his personal travel account "Sofia - portrait of a city", which until today has remained one of few internationally available books on contemporary Sofia[1]. Almost a decade later and despite its membership in the EU, labels like "unknown" and "unfamiliar" still seem to hold true. Bulgaria´s image in the West is still fused with stereotypes about "the Balkans" as a peripheral – and potentially dangerous – "Other", in contrast to the perceived core of Europe (Brunnbauer n. d., Todorova 1994, 1997). In this imagery, contemporary cities and urban life hardly figure at all.

A central task of anthropology is to bring the unfamiliar into focus. The papers in this book are based on short-term student research projects in a fieldwork training excursion in 2010. It is obvious that such short studies cannot replace a comprehensive urban ethnography of Sofia, but they aim to contribute to a better understanding of Sofia as a major city in contemporary Europe.

Sofia: urban space in historical development

Although relatively young as the capital of Bulgaria, Sofia looks back on a venerable history. In Thracian and Roman times, the ancient Serdica (Сердика) was already an urban centre of major importance, while traces of human habitation date back much longer. In the Roman period, the city became "*an important link in the* diagonis *connecting Rome with its far-flung eastern territories*" (Staddon, Mollov 2000: 380). This central

1 A comprehensive publication on Sofia in English was published in 2001 for the 120th anniversary as capital of Bulgaria (Bulgarian Academy of Sciences et al. 2001), but this massive volume is no longer in stock.

location on the crossroads between East and West also ensured its position in the Byzantine Empire and in the first and second Bulgarian Kingdoms, when the city was called "Sredets" (Средец). In 1382, Ottoman troops conquered the city which at that time was already named "Sofia" (Holy Wisdom). During the subsequent Ottoman rule, Sofia became an important garrison and a node of trade and administration (Staddon, Mollov 2000; Bulgarian Academy of Sciences et al. 2001). During the 18th and 19th centuries, Sofia evolved into a major location for international trade and industry, with an estimated population exceeding 11 000 around 1850 (Dimitrov 2001) and a growing urban infrastructure (Gavrilova 2009).

View of Ottoman Sofia: the market street (улица Търговска) opposite Bania Bashi Camii. Watercolour painting by Joseph Oberbauer[2] (Fileva et al. 2010)

2 The oeuvre of Joseph Oberbauer (1854-1926), an Austrian architect who was employed as chief draftsman of the Sofia Municipal Council, shows impressions of pre-Liberation Sofia as an Ottoman city. In meticulous drawings and small water-

Shortly after the Liberation in 1878, the number of inhabitants had risen to more than 20 000 (Hristov 2001: 78). The original layout of the city was massively altered to accommodate its new functions as national capital and a steadily increasing population (Gavrilova 2003, 2009). Except for single buildings of historic value such as the former *Büyük Camii,* now housing the Archaeological Museum, or the *Bania Bashi Camii* which is still used as a mosque, few traces of Ottoman Sofia have remained.

Following the example of Vienna, Sofia was redesigned along a pattern of concentric circles dominated by a ring boulevard, which contained its major functions and the more prestigious residential quarters (Staddon, Mollov 2000, Stancheva 2001). This new, "European" ground plan was complemented by the adaptation of Western building styles ranging from neo-classical to Art Nouveau.

Historic postcard depicting the street opposite Bania Bashi Camii, early 20th century. The former Ottoman market street (see above) has been replaced by

colour paintings, he documented views of the city before it was transformed into a modern capital (Fileva et al. 2010).

Western-style storefront buildings. The Central Market Halls (централни хали), designed by Naum Torbov in a neo-byzantine style matching the Synagogue behind it, were opened in 1911 (private collection, W.K.).

Leading architects like Petko Momchilov (1864-1923) and Friedrich Grünanger (1856-1929) created a unique style for representative buildings such as the Mineral Baths (1904-05) or the central Synagogue, by combining Orientalist and Art Nouveau elements in the dominating colours yellow and red (Dobreva 2010, Doytchinov, Gantchev 2001, Roth 1989).

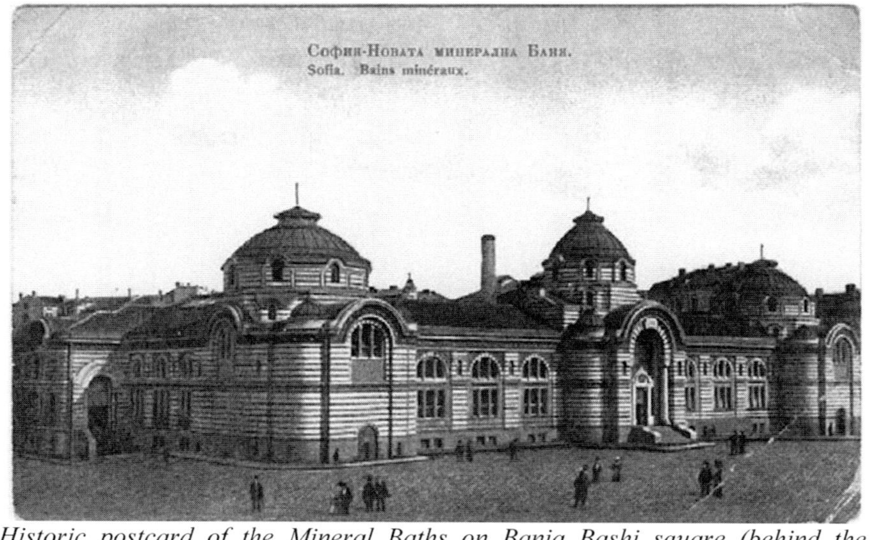

Historic postcard of the Mineral Baths on Bania Bashi square (behind the mosque), early 20th century. The baths were designed by Petko Momchilov and Friedrich Grünanger (1904-1905) in a style combining Orientalist, neo-Byzantine and Viennese Secessionist elements (private collection, W.K.).

The first decades of the 20th century saw new waves of immigration from rural areas, attracted by Sofia´s rapid industrial expansion, as well as refugees from Rumelia and Macedonia. By 1920, the number of inhabitants had risen to more than 150 000 (Hristov 2001). New residential quarters for the poorer segments of the population were developed in the western areas of town, surrounded by industry and by uncharted dwellings of Roma and of other groups considered as undesirable. The socio-spatial layering of the city was even reflected in the ground plan of the new central cemetery, which was opened in 1889 in the village Orlandovtsi (Орландовци). Here, graves were grouped together following the same principles of social differentiation, religious affiliation and kinship. Interestingly, this social differentiation was maintained even during the times of state socialism (Yaneva 2001).

Of German origin (Saxe-Coburg-Gotha), the Bulgarian tsars Ferdinand (1861-1948) and Boris III (1894-1943) had maintained strong cultural and political relations to Germany and Western Europe. German influence on Bulgaria increased during the 1930^{es}. In World War II, Bulgaria was allied with Germany[3] as it had initially been in World War I. In 1944, Sofia was bombarded by Allied troops, resulting in massive damages to industrial areas and to parts of the city centre (Staddon, Mollov 2000).

After 1944, Bulgaria was incorporated into the Communist bloc. Georgi Dimitrov remained the leading figure in Bulgarian politics until his death in 1949, followed by Todor Shivkov (1911-1998) as Party General Secretary. Following the example of Lenin, Dimitrovs dead body was preserved and exhibited in a mausoleum in the centre of Sofia, facing the former royal palace. The destruction of this monument in 1989 became a massively contested symbol of the changes after the end of the Communist era (Knaus 1997: 24 f.). Recently, this place has been used by

3 Until 1943, more than 23 000 Jews, mainly of Sephardic origin, had lived in Sofia playing a significant role in the city´s history and development. In summer of 1943, the Jews of Sofia were to be deported to the concentration camps, but due to massive protests from politicians, Church officials and concerned citizens these plans were delayed and eventually abandoned (more than 11 000 Jews from other areas of Bulgaria were however deported). This chapter of Bulgaria´s history is still relatively unknown in Western Europe and it remains contested, as historians disagree on the role of the government, particularly of Tsar Boris III (Haskell 1994, Luleva 2010, Trankova, Georgieff 2011: 26 ff).

an independent Christian church for celebrating mass in a semi-permanent tent.

From 1944 to 1989, city planning in Sofia reflected the ambitions of the Communist party. The old core of the city retained its major administrative functions, while a great part of the surrounding residential quarters built in the late 19th and early 20th centuries fell into disrepair. New suburbs were planned to accommodate the rising influx of industrial workers to Sofia. These residential districts, consisting of huge blocks of high-rise apartment buildings, were designed as self-contained communities with administrative sub-centres, shopping malls or markets, schools and even universities. Between 1945 and 1975, the number of Sofia's inhabitants increased to more than one million (Hristov 2001, National Statistical Institute 2011).

Apartment block in the residential quarter Nadeshda (photo: K. de Jong 2009)

The leading position which Bulgaria´s industry had achieved among the states of the Warsaw pact following a phase of forced industrialization, ended abruptly after 1989. With the demise of the Soviet Union, Bulgarian exports had lost their main recipient. On a globalized market, Bulgarian industrial products were no longer competitive (Knaus 1997: 113). When imports of petrol from Russia ceased in 1990, Bulgaria´s economy suffered a dramatic decline, leading to a breakdown of the financial system and to severe shortages of supplies. Since 2001, Bulgaria´s economy has been growing at a rate of 5% p.a., to a large degree due to foreign capital (Grimm-Pretner, Rode 2007: 12), but incomes still rank among the lowest in the EU[4].

The massive social and economic changes in Bulgaria after 1989 are clearly reflected in Sofia´s urban space. Officially, the population amounts to over 1 270 000, but due to unregistered migration, factual numbers are estimated to be much higher (NSI 2011). The presence of private vehicles has increased dramatically, resulting in permanent traffic jams, air pollution and in the transformation of most free spaces into parking lots. Billboards and advertisements are virtually everywhere. Buildings and monuments symbolically related to the socialist past have been "*subjected to a process between tolerated degradation and conscious destruction. The cultural semantics of space have been replaced by the semantics of a market-economy*" (Grimm-Pretner, Rode 2007:11[5]).

Following banking and trade, real estate development has become the third strongest sector of foreign investments (Grimm-Pretner, Rode 2007:12). While some of the Art Nouveau buildings in the central districts are currently being renovated and transformed into hotels,

---

4 http://www.welt.de/wirtschaft/article931619/In_Bulgarien_kostet_eine_Arbeitsstunde_1_80_Euro.html

5 Original in German (transl. by W. Kokot): "Die Orte mit hoher Symbolkraft für die Ära des Sozialismus unterliegen einem Prozess zwischen geduldeter Abwertung und absichtlicher Zerstörung. Die kulturelle Lesart des Raums wird durch eine marktwirtschaftliche Lesart ersetzt."

restaurants or luxury shops, large parts of the old residential quarters outside the inner ring are still in a state of decay, reflecting an increasing rate of urban poverty[6]. Residential quarters formerly reserved for the party elite, mostly located in the southern areas of the city, have become sites of private development reflecting upper-middle aspirations, while gated luxury apartment blocks reserved for the new rich are rapidly built in the outskirts, close to the mountains.

Pirotska Street, a popular shopping area in central Sofia (photo: W. Kokot 2010)

In the high-rise suburbs built in socialist times, privatization of formerly common space such as parks or playgrounds has led to unregulated construction of small stores, workshops and even condominiums between

6 According to the National Statistical Institute, the average household income in Bulgaria in 2011 is 940 Leva (470 €) with consumer prices reaching European levels in many sectors (NSI 2011). For 2009, EU reports state that 20% of the Bulgarian population were living below the poverty threshold (www.euractiv.de).

the older apartment blocks (Grimm-Pretner, Rode 2007:13 ff.). Along the thoroughfares leading through these suburbs, new shopping centres emerge along with fast food chain restaurants. A large Chinese shopping mall in the quarter of Nadeshda demonstrates the presence of new immigrants, who also leave their mark on the urban environment (Kristeva 2005).

Ethnographic research in Bulgaria

As in other European countries, the history of ethnography in Bulgaria has been closely related to political aspirations of the nation state (Benovska-Sabkova 2007, 2010, Elchinova 2008). In the years before and after 1878, ethnography or folklore studies were directed at documenting and "reviving" elements of Bulgarian traditions, in clear contrast to all traces of Ottoman culture (Roth 1989). During socialism, ethnographic research was once more limited to "folk traditions" within Bulgaria, as fieldwork in foreign countries was virtually impossible due to ideological as well as financial limitations.

In recent years, processes of political, social and economic transformation form a distinct focus of research on contemporary Bulgaria. In this field, ethnographic research offers important insights about the effects of these changes on a local level. In this discussion, recent studies by Bulgarian ethnographers have been of particular importance (Benovska-Sabkova 2007, 2010), complementing surveys and overviews on a nationwide scale (e.g. Center for the study of democracy 2010, Genov 2010).

In summary, the picture presented by ethnographic research on the local level is much more differentiated than the tenor of general pessimism which is presented in surveys and general studies on the macro level. This is particularly visible in recent research focusing on trust and on the uses of social capital (Giordano 2008, Roth ed. 2007) in friendship and leisure groups (Benovska-Sabkova 2008) or at the work place (Benovska-Sabkova 2004, Roth ed. 2004, Petrova 2007). The significance of social networks has also been highlighted in the case of new entrepreneurs (Giordano 2010), or of mutual support between villagers and city dwellers (Barova 2008 a). As Giordano (2010) has argued, the strategic uses of social networks may also be seen as an asset not only for economic development, but also for the emergence of civil society institutions on a grassroots level[7].

Although many of the themes in current studies are related to an urban context, explicit references to urban anthropology are still rare[8], although Gavrilova (2003, 2009) and others have provided valuable insights into the historical development of Sofia´s urban culture in the 18th and 19th century. For contemporary Sofia, most ethnographic studies have focused on particular phenomena, e.g. youth culture (Barova 2004, 2008 b) or certain diaspora communities (e.g. Haskell 1994, Kokot 2009). With very few exceptions (e.g. Ditchev 2006), an explicit ethnography of Sofia as such is still missing. Although the studies presented in this book do not aspire to fill this gap, they aim to add further aspects to the overall picture of Sofia´s urban culture(s).

Student fieldwork in Sofia 2010

For students majoring in Social Anthropology (*Ethnologie*) at the University of Hamburg, fieldwork training is a core part of the curriculum. While the majority of students choose individual field projects, organized group excursions are also offered at regular intervals. Besides in-depth mentoring during all phases of research, these excursions offer the added opportunity to relate the students´ fieldwork to the teaching staff's actual

---

7 In this context, Grimm-Pretner and Rode (2007:14) mention the emergence of citizens´ resistance against the privatization and re-utilization of parks and common free space in Mladost. Starting from a loose association of concerned neighbours, the movement was registered as NGO in 2002. Until 2006, 40 such organizations had been founded, merging into the organization "Green Sofia" (see also Höpfner in this volume).

8 although Roth ed. (2005) contains several articles on Bulgarian cities.

research projects and interests (Kokot 2007, Mischung in pr., Wonneberger 2011).

Urban anthropology has been a focus of research and teaching at our institute for nearly two decades. Accordingly, several fieldwork training excursions have also taken place in an urban context, e. g. Thessaloniki in 2004 (Kokot 2007) or Dublin in 2006 (Wonneberger 2011). In 2010, we chose Sofia as our field site, because it offers a wide range of topics closely related to major areas of research in our institute, such as diaspora and migration, post-socialist transformation, urban social networks and everyday economic strategies.

The choice of Sofia was also based on ongoing academic cooperation with Bulgarian colleagues, as well as on my own earlier fieldwork in the context of diaspora studies (Kokot 2009). First preparations for the excursion started in winter term of 2009/10, with an introductory seminar on the ethnography of Bulgaria and seminars on research design and methodology. Preparations were intensified in summer term of 2010, with all participants designing their individual projects. Guest lectures by Bulgarian colleagues complemented these seminars. At the same time, the students were involved in the editorial work on an issue of the journal *Ethnoscripts* focusing on ethnology in Bulgaria (Kokot ed. 2010). During the whole year, the students took a self-organized language course offered by one of the participants, who is a native speaker of Bulgarian.

The core fieldwork period lasted from September 1 until mid-October 2010, while some participants decided to stay longer. Different from the usual course of fieldwork trainings, this project was designed to include both German and Bulgarian researchers. A group of graduate students was brought together by Milena Benovska-Sabkova in Sofia and first contacts were established by e-mail before we entered the field. In Sofia, the fieldwork period was structured by weekly seminars on research design and methodology, which also served as a platform to discuss preliminary results and potential problems with our Bulgarian partners. The initial plan to include the Bulgarian students in the actual fieldwork process did not work out, because as graduates on doctoral or postdoctoral levels, they were already deeply immersed in their own research projects. However, they acted as mentors and expert informants for the German group on questions of Bulgarian culture and inside knowledge about Sofia, as well as discussing their own research interests and contributing important contacts.

To establish first contacts with potential informants is a major challenge of fieldwork in big cities. As most students had already started communication with relevant institutions or individuals via e-mail in advance, finding an entry into the field was not a big problem in most cases. In Sofia, the Bulgarian partners also helped to establish initial contacts which were then extended through a snowball system.

Finding accommodation was a different issue however. In Sofia, there is a general shortage of affordable living space. Although there is a specialized market offering apartments to foreign sojourners, the rents are forbiddingly high. In our case, all accommodations had to be booked far in advance via internet and/or with the help of personal contacts. Consequently, the group was spread throughout the city. Only two students shared an apartment, while Eleonora Wewer stayed with her parents outside of Sofia and commuted to her urban field every day. This rather exhausting procedure was necessary because as a mother of two small children, she saw no other way to combine fieldwork and family obligations.

Our weekly seminars hosted by the International Foundation St. Cyril and Methodius in a central location on Vasil Aprilov Street, became the most important platform for exchange within the group. Besides these weekly meetings, I met all students in their field sites for individual discussions and supervision of their progress. Regular contact within the group was also ensured though individual meetings and ongoing exchange by e-mail.

Language was a particular problem in this excursion. While Eleonora Wewer and Ivan Raduychev are native speakers of Bulgarian, the other students had no prior knowledge of the language and, with one exception, no contacts to Bulgaria at all. Except for Mascha Kern, who is a native speaker of Russian, learning Bulgarian in the short time span available posed considerable difficulties. Consequently, most topics were chosen in such a way that interviews could be conducted in English, German or in Russian. Nonetheless, learning the language to at least a modest level is an absolute prerequisite for field work, also in training situations. In this excursion, the participants′ basic knowledge of Bulgarian proved invaluable not only for managing necessities like everyday shopping, but also for establishing first contacts and facilitating initial acceptance by the informants, as a sign of respect for their language and culture.

A detailed research report (30-50 pages) is part of the requirements for all fieldwork training excursions. Only after the report has been accepted, the fieldwork training is considered as successfully completed. After returning from the field, the next tasks were the evaluation of field data and the design and writing of the final reports. Based on the common research outline developed before the field period, a set of categories was defined for data evaluation and applied (using the program Atlas ti for all qualitative data)[9]. In a seminar in winter 2010/11, a common guideline for structuring the reports was developed and the seminar served as a writers′ workshop, so all reports were finished in time. Still in the field, the whole group had decided to aim for a publication of the results following the examples of earlier excursions. From summer of 2011 until the beginning of winter 2011/12, all participants were busy with writing the articles for this collection on the basis of their final reports. All papers have been revised several times during this process.Field methods and basic data

Although some topics required the additional use of specific methods, a general methodological framework was developed for all participants, together with a set of basic questions which were to be answered in all cases. An important aim of the fieldwork training program is to apply a wide range of ethnographic methods in an actual field situation, so besides observation (participant and non-participant) and different types

9 www.atlasti.com/de

of interviews, students were also required to gather basic demographic information, data on semantic domains, on social networks and mental maps representing the informants´ knowledge of the urban space of Sofia.

Not surprisingly, observation and (narrative) interviews form the major part of the data collected in the field. In contrast, applying more standardized elicitation techniques such as free listing or mental mapping proved difficult in many cases. One the one hand, some informants did not agree to formal elicitation procedures or lost interest too quickly. On the other hand and despite all attempts at teaching methodology systematically[10], most students still were conspicuously hesitant to apply formal methods in the field, either for fear of intruding on the informants, or because they still did not feel adequately familiar with these techniques[11].

Nonetheless, a core of comparable data was collected in all cases, including basic demographic information on all persons who had either been formally interviewed or involved in longer discussions or in major observations. In total, 96 persons are included in the field sample[12].

Gender ratio

With 51,3 % f vs. 48,7% m, the gender ratio in our sample is even slightly more balanced than data from the 2011 national census (56,3% f vs.43,7% m) would suggest (NSI 2011). This is somewhat surprising, as except for one male student, all participants in this excursion were

10 A series of regular courses on different methods, ranging from qualitative to quantitative approaches, are an obligatory part of the course of studies at the Hamburg institute (compare Lang 2002).

11 Similar problem arose already during the fieldwork training excursion to Thessaloniki (Kokot ed. 2007:20 f.). Astrid Wonneberger (2011: 20) also reports difficulties in the application of standardized methods in her field excursion to Dublin. A solution has yet to be found – more practice before entering the field is advisable at any rate.

12 Hartmut Lang has provided invaluable help in analyzing the following demographic data.

women. However, most topics were not explicitly gender-specific, except for Katharina Kunze´s study on a women´s NGO, and to a certain degree also Mascha Kern´s research among Russian dancers.

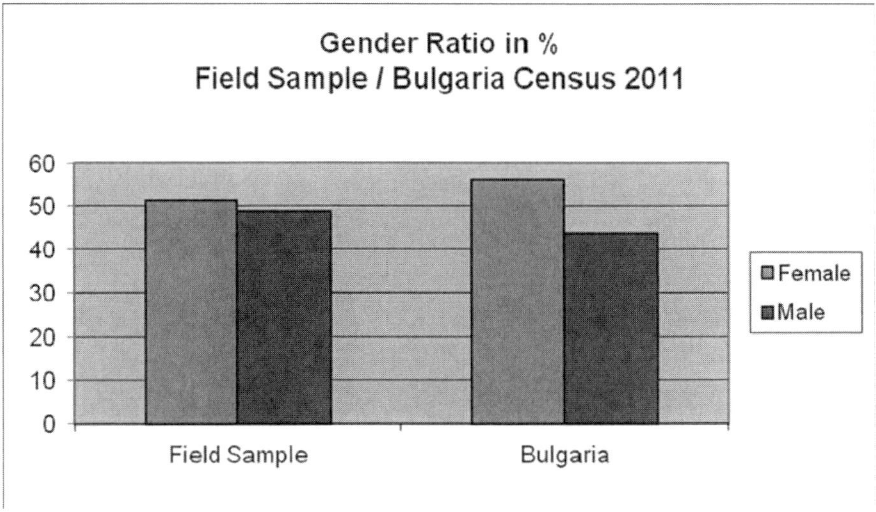

Table 1: gender ratio, field sample / census 2011

Age distribution

As on gender, no specific data on age categories were available for Sofia alone, so in the following tables or sample is compared to overall data on Bulgaria in general. Here, age is categorized as children below 15, adults between 15 and 65, and elderly over 65 years.

In our sample, no children below 15 years were included, versus 17% in the Bulgarian population. Almost all of our informants (93%) belong to the category of adults (vs. 68% in the total population), while the ratio of elderly informants (7%) is lower than in the total population (11%).

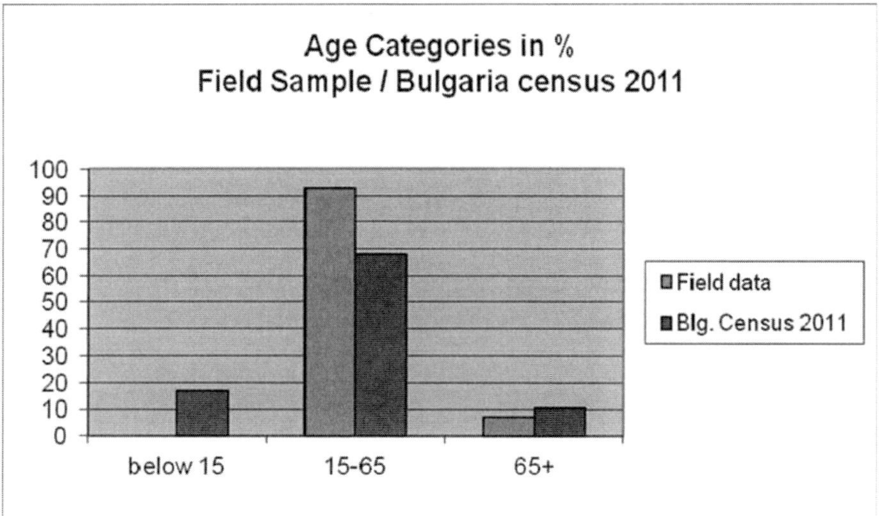

Table 2: Age categories, field sample / census 2011

Considering the distribution of age categories, our sample obviously reflects the preference of student ethnographers for informants of their own generation. This picture becomes even clearer when the category of adults is differentiated further. As the following table shows, while few informants (2%) below 20 years were included, the sample shows a clear predominance of the age bracket between 21 and 40 (51%), followed by the bracket between 41 and 60 (40%). Only 7% of the informants were older than 60 years.

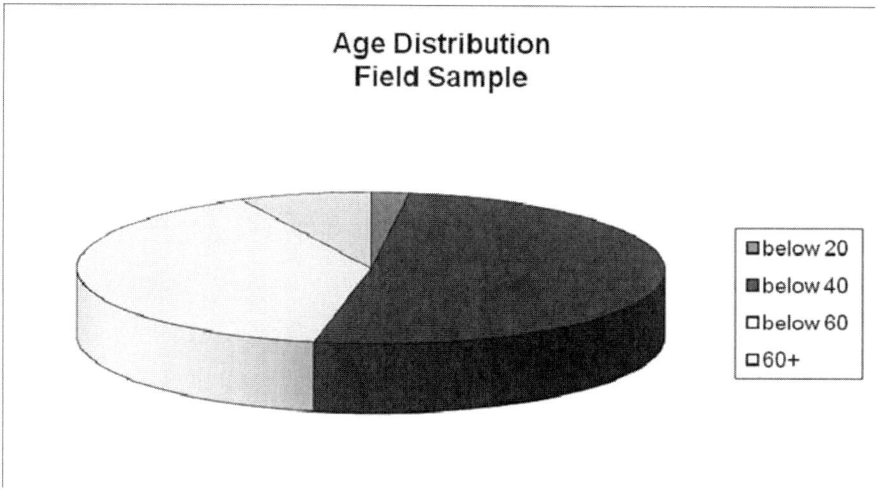

Table 3: Age distribution, field sample

Educational level

General levels of education in Bulgaria are relatively high. According to the 2011 census, more than half of the population (56, 2%) have finished secondary education, while 23, 2% have graduated from the tertiary level (university, technical university etc.). Even considering this ratio however, our sample[13] shows an obvious academic bias. Only 4% of our informants (vs. 20, 6% in the total population) had finished their schooling after primary level[14] and 34% had finished with secondary education. The overwhelming majority of our sample (62 %) were either currently studying at, or had graduated from universities.

13 Seven persons gave no information and were omitted from the sample for this issue.

14 Special education for learning disabilities or for the handicapped are included here.

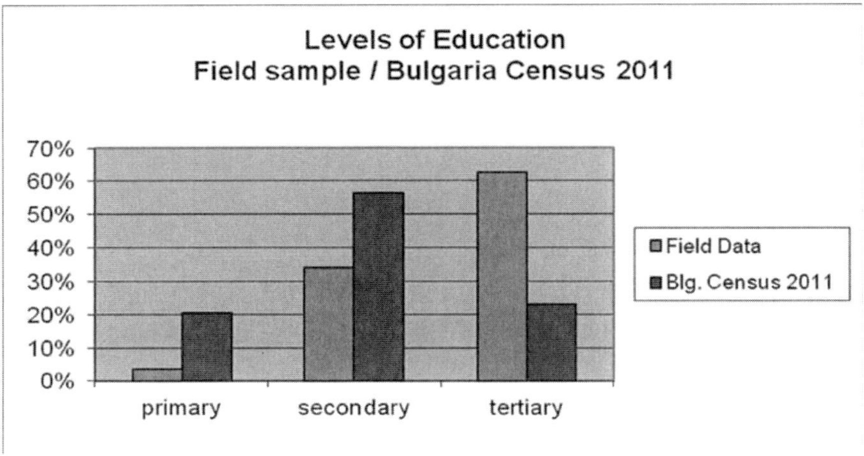

Table 4: Levels of education, field sample / census 2011

Professions

Considering the economic realities in Bulgaria today, it is not surprising that the professions named by our informants as their major source of income do not always reflect their educational standard. A comparison with general data on Bulgaria was not possible here, as no data on comparable categories were available. In this case, a comparison would probably also make not much sense, since the distribution of professions is clearly biased by the topics of the individual research projects. Nonetheless, the following table presents an overview over the variety of professions and livelihood strategies pursued by our informants.

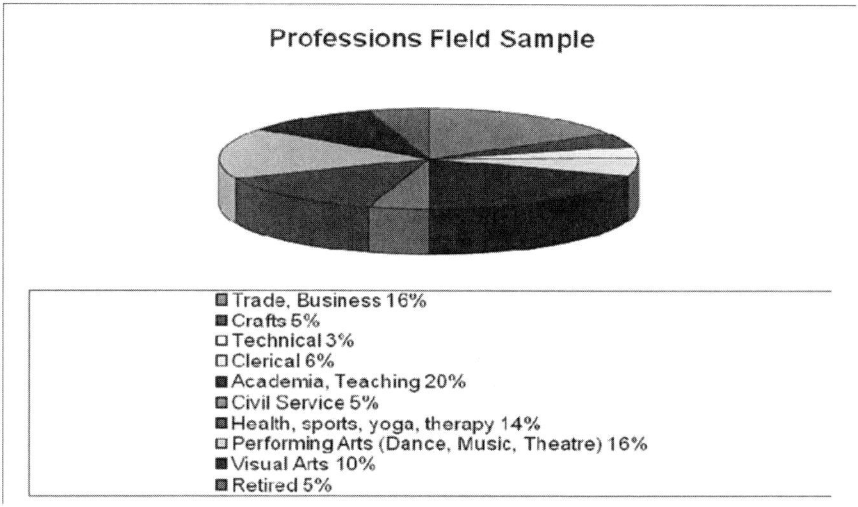

Table 5: Professions, field sample

The papers in this volume

The seven projects presented here cover a variety of topics derived from the students´ individual interests. Nonetheless, they also address common themes linked to current ethnological research about Bulgaria.

In her study on Russian speaking dancers in Sofia, Mascha Kern discusses the significance of diaspora networks and institutions in terms of social and cultural capital. With these topics, her paper relates to theses about the meaning of social capital and trust in Bulgaria (Giordano 2008, Roth ed. 2007), and to recent research on diasporas at our institute[15]

The management of social relations and their significance for spreading new and alternative value systems are the topic of Ivan Raduychev´s research in a Sofia yoga community. Despite political pressures in communist times, the founder of the group managed to establish a small but effective core of trustful relations which helped her disseminate her teachings and which still is an important basis of her work.

Strong social relations also form a significant resource for the success of a well-established womens´ NGO studied by Katharina Kunze. With her observations, she confirms existing research on the importance of friendship and social exchange at the workplace. In contrast to prevailing views of private relations on the workplace as a problem, her study underlines their importance as a resource for successful project management.

Non-government organizations and emerging institutions of civil society (Hackmann, Roth (eds.) 2011) are also the theme of Mira Höpfner´s paper. Using the example of environmentalism, her study focuses on civil involvement among Bulgaria´s younger generation. In line with Giordano´s (2010) arguments, she presents a moderately optimistic view of the future of civil society in Bulgaria.

---

15. http://www.uni-hamburg.de/ethnologie/diaspores_e.html

Local effects of large-scale economic change can be observed particularly clearly in the case of small enterprises, which form a major part of Bulgaria´s post-transition economy (Bartlett, Rangelova 1997). In her comparison of two small cafés in Sofia, Renate Kleinknecht discusses the management of daily work routines and the uses of social relations on the workplace.

Young independent artists represent two contrasting currents in contemporary Bulgaria. On the one hand, they embody a new freedom to choose alternative lifestyles suited for creative work. On the other hand, many of them live in extremely precarious conditions, after state subsidies and institutions supporting the arts have ceased to exist. Consequently, a major focus of Sinnika Harm´s search for an "art scene" in Sofia is on the artists´ economic situation and on their livelihood strategies.

Comparable, but even more dramatic, is the situation of street musicians in Sofia. As Eleonora Wewer shows, many of them not only live and perform under extremely precarious conditions, but they are also still subjected to old prejudices and social stigmatization based on ethnic stereotypes and the social exclusion of "vagrant" professions.

Following their work on this volume, most of the authors are currently preparing their M.A. theses on topics developed out of the excursion. Two authors have returned to Sofia for further fieldwork in the meantime and a third follow-up study is planned for 2012. For all of us, Sofia will remain a fascinating city presenting a wealth of issues for future research.

References

Barova, Vihra (2004): Mladejkite subkulturi v Bulgaria prez 80-te I nachaloto na 90-te godini na 20 vek. - [Youth subcultures in Bulgaria during 80's and early 90's of 20th century] Bulgarska etnologia [Bulgarian Ethnology] 30, 1: 92-100.

— (2008 a) A Bulgarian Example of Exchange and Reciprocity in the Family. Halle/Saale: Max Planck Inst. for Social Anthropology: Working Papers 102.

— (2008 b) Post-socialist Punk Identity: From Dissidents to Workers. In: Schröder, I. W., A. Vonderau (eds.) (2008) Changing Economies and Changing Identities in Postsocialist Eastern Europe. Münster, Wien, Berlin.

Bartlett, Will and Rossitsa Rangelova (1997) Small Firms and Economic Transformation in Bulgaria. Small Business Economics, 9: 319-333.

Benovska-Sabkova, Milena (2004) Social Networks, Coalitions and Clientelism at the Workplace in Bulgaria. In: Roth, Klaus (ed.): Arbeit im Sozialismus- Arbeit im Postsozialismus. Münster, Wien, Berlin: 109-128.

— (2007) Anthropology and related disciplines: the view from Bulgaria. In: Hann, Chris (ed.) (2004) Anthropology's multiple temporalities and its future in Central and Eastern Europe. Halle/Saale: Max Planck Institute for Social Anthropology: 11-14.

— (2008) Leisure Time, Friendship Groups and Social Capital in Bulgaria. Examples from Socialist and Postsocialist Period. In: Roth, Klaus (ed.) (2008): 183-204.

— (2010) Bulgarian Ethnology in the Wake of 1989: Expanding Horizons, Challenging Frontiers. In: Kokot (ed.) (2010): 181-217.

Brunnbauer, Ulf (n.d.) "Europa" und der "Balkan". Fremd- und Selbstzuschreibungen. Berlin: FU Osteuropa-Institut, Vorlesung „Einführung in die Geschichte Südosteuropas". http://userpage.fu-berlin.de/~ulf/Europa%20und%20der%20Balkan.pdf

Bulgarian Academy of Sciences, Municipality of Sofia (eds.) (2001) Sofia. 120 years as capital of Bulgaria. Sofia.

Center for the Study of Democracy (2010) Civil Society in Bulgaria. Trends and Risks. Sofia.

Dimitrov, Strashimir (2001) Sofia in the eighteenth century. In: Bulgarian Academy of Sciences et al. (eds.) (2001): 170-180.

Ditchev, Ivaylo (2006) Sofia, fluid city. Dérive- Zeitschrift für Stadtforschung, 6 (repr. http://www.eurozine.com/articles/article_2007-05-25-ditchev-de.html).

Dobreva, Doroteya (2010) Images of the Own – Images of the Other. Bulgaria's Presentation through the Fine Arts at the 1900 World Exhibition in Paris. In: Kokot (ed.) (2010): 136-150.

Doytchinov, Grigor; Christo Gantchev (2001) Österreichische Architekten in Bulgarien 1878-1918. Wien, Köln, Weimar.

Elchinova, Magdalena (2008) Sociocultural Anthropology in Bulgaria: Desired and Contested. In: Boskovic, Aleksandar (ed.) (2008) Other People's Anthropologies: Ethnographic Practice on the Margins. Oxford, New York: 70-83.

Fileva, Adelina; Boris Chilev; Krassimir Iliev (2010) Josef Oberbauer 1854-1926: sledite na grada [traces of the town]. Sofia: Sofia City Art Gallery Exhibition Catalogue.

Gavrilova, Raina (2003) Orte, Ansichten und Zeichen: Die Herausbildung des öffentlichen Raumes im städtischen Millieu. In: Heppner, Harald; Roumania Preshlenova (eds.) (2003) Öffentlichkeit ohne Tradition. Bulgariens Aufbruch in die Moderne. Frankfurt Main et. al.: 167-191.

— (2009) Bulgarian Urban Culture in the Eighteenth and Nineteenth Centuries. Selinsgrove, London.

Genov, Nikolai (2010) Ups and Downs of Social Democracy in Bulgaria. Sofia: Friedrich Ebert Foundation Office, Bulgaria Analyses.

Giordano, Christian (2007) Privates Vertrauen und informelle Netzwerke: zur Organisationskultur in Gesellschaften öffentlichen Misstrauens. Südosteuropa im Blickpunkt. In: Roth, Klaus (ed.) (2007): 21-50.

— (2008) Sozialkapital aus anthropologischer Sicht. Eine kritische Betrachtung. In: Roth, Klaus (ed.) (2008): 33-52.

— (2010) Why New Agrarian Capitalists are Successful in Bulgaria: The Relevance of Personalized Social Networks and Face to Face Trust Relations. In: Kokot (ed.) (2010): 15-33.

Grimm-Pretner, Dagmar; Philipp Rode 2007: Stadtlaboratorium Sofia. Beobachtungen zur postsozialistischen Stadtentwicklung. Dérive – Zeitschrift für Stadtforschung, 26: 11-15.

Hackmann, Jörg; Klaus Roth (eds.) (2011): Zivilgesellschaft im östlichen und südöstlichen Europa in Geschichte und Gegenwart. München.

Haskell, Guy H. (1994) From Sofia to Jaffa. The Jews of Bulgaria and Israel. Detroit.

Hristov, Emil (2001) Demographic Development. In: Bulgarian Academy of Sciences et al. (eds.) (2001): 78-82.

Kokot, Waltraud (ed.) (2007) Beyond the White Tower – Transformations in Thessaloniki. Münster, Wien, Berlin: lines, vol. 4.

Kokot, Waltraud (2010) Ethnologie in Bulgarien: Forschungsfeld und Fachentwicklung. In: Kokot (ed.) (2010): 3-14.

— (ed.) (2010) Ethnologie Bulgariens - Bulgarische Ethnologie? Hamburg: Ethnoscripts. Analysen und Informationen aus dem Institut für Ethnologie der Universität Hamburg, 12,1.

— (2009) Diaspora as a Resource? Managing Social Capital in the Armenian Community of Sofia, Bulgaria. In: Greiner, Clemens; Waltraud Kokot (Hg.): (2009) Networks, resources and economic action: ethnographic case studies in honour of Hartmut Lang. Berlin: 127-150.

Knaus, Gerald (1997) Bulgarien. München: Beck´sche Reihe Länder.

Kristeva, Anna (2005) Kitaizite [the Chinese]. In: Kristeva, Anna (ed.) (2005) Immigraziata v Bulgaria [Immigration to Bulgaria}. Sofia: 80-104.

Lang, Hartmut (2002) Vorbemerkungen zum Lehrveranstaltungszyklus "Methoden der Ethnographie" am Hamburger Institut für Ethnologie. Hamburg: Ethnoscripts. Analysen und Informationen aus dem Institut für Ethnologie der Universität Hamburg 4,1: 162-165.

Luleva, Ana (2010) Politics of memory in post-socialist Bulgaria. In: Kokot (ed.) (2010): 77-92.

Mischung, Roland (in preparation): Living in a Modern Karen Village. Münster, Wien, Berlin, lines.

NSI (2011) National Statistical Institute of Bulgaria, www.nsi.bg.

Petrova, Ivanka (2007) Männervertrauen – Frauenvertrauen in der Arbeitswelt. In: Roth (ed.) (2007): 303-316.

Roth, Klaus (1989) Osmanische Spuren in der Alltagskultur Südosteuropas. In: Majer, Hans-Georg (ed.) (1989) Die Staaten Südosteuropas und die Osmanen. München: Südosteuropa-Jahrbuch 19: 319-332.

— (ed.) (2004) Arbeit im Sozialismus – Arbeit im Postsozialismus. Erkundungen zum Arbeitsleben im östlichen Europa. Münster, Wien, Berlin: 109-128.

— (ed.) (2005) Urban Life and Culture in Southeastern Europe. München: Ethnologia Balkanica. Journal for Southeast European Anthropology, 9.

— (2007) Trust; Networks and Social Capital in the Transformation Countries. Ethnological Perspectives. In: Roth (ed.) (2007): 7-20.

— (ed.) (2007) Soziale Netzwerke und soziales Vertrauen in den Transformationsländern. Münster, Wien, Berlin.

— (ed.) (2008) Sozialkapital – Vertrauen – Rechtssichertheit. Zürich, Berlin: Freiburger Sozialanthropologische Studien, 19.

Staddon, Caedmon; Bellin Mollov (2000) City Profile: Sofia, Bulgaria. Cities, 17, 5: 379-387.

Stancheva, Magdalina (2001) The town: from Serdonpolis to Sofia. In: Bulgarian Academy of Sciences et al. (eds.) (2001): 124-137.

Todorova, Maria (1994) The Balkans: From Discovery to Invention. Slavic Review, 53, 2: 453–482.

— (1997) Imagining the Balkans. New York, Oxford.

Trankova, Dimana; Anthony Georgieff (2011 A guide to Jewish Bulgaria. Sofia.

Ward, Philip (1993) Sofia. Portrait of a City. Cambridge, New York City.

Wonneberger, Astrid (2011) Cultural Contrasts in Dublin. A Montage of Ethnographic Studies. Münster, Wien, Berlin: lines, vol. 6.

Yaneva, Stanka (2001) The other town. On the structure of the central cemetery of Sofia. Ethnologia Bulgaria 2: 111-116.

Mobility and resources in the performing arts: Russian-speaking dancers in Sofia

Mascha Kern

> "Commonly, dance is rather considered a leisure time activity. (...) Due to the current politico-economic situation of the country, it is hard to establish dance as profession in Bulgaria these days. (...) It is (...) not profitable."[1],

With these words, Viktorija[2], a dance instructor, described her situation during an interview in a dressing room, while her pupils were practicing the new choreography. According to Viktorija, the economic instability in Bulgaria after the fall of socialism has led to a changing attitude towards the arts as a profession. In present times, parents would rather invest in other areas of education they think more profitable for their children in the future.

This paper focuses on the diverse resources mobilized by Russian-speaking dancers in their professional lives. Recently, the sector of "creative professions" has been discussed as an economic factor, as well as an asset in the competition between cities (Barber-Kersovan 2007: 11). During the six weeks of my fieldwork, I investigated dance as a creative profession in Sofia, focusing in particular on Russian-speaking migrants or descendants of migrants, who were professional dancers. Based on the concept of social and cultural *embeddedness* of economic actions (Gebesmair 2009:157, Kloostermann; Rath 2001), the actors' social and cultural resources were central points of my interest. In order to determine the role of ethnic networks, I also investigated the organization and structure of the Russian-speaking community in Sofia.

---

1 „Танец, по общему мнению, это всего лишь развлечение. (…) В настоящее время в Болгарии танец как профессию развивать очень сложно из-за политико-финансовой ситуации в стране. (…) Это (…) не рентабельно" (Interview 41, Viktoria, 2.10.2010 [translation: M.K.]).

2 In this paper, all informants are referred to by pseudonyms to ensure their anonymity.

Basic data

My primary aim was to gather basic information about Russians living in Sofia as a context for my core research group, the Russian-speaking dancers. During the initial phase of the fieldwork, regular visits to the Russian Cultural Centre in Sofia[3] provided general information about the Russian community. I attended some cultural events organized by this institution where I met one key informant. Contacting more informants by a snowball system proved unsuccessful however, as the main actors did not seem to interact with each other. The other informants were gathered through visiting different dance institutions.

The Russian Cultural Centre in central Sofia (photo: M. Kern)

3 Российский культурно-информационный центр.

At large, I interviewed 12 persons (3 m, 9 f) about the topics "Russian diaspora" or/and "dance". One person provided expert information, as he is a historian specialised on Russian history working at the Bulgarian Academy of Sciences. Only two dancers were able to answer questions about the Russian diaspora or the Russian community in Sofia. All interviewed dancers were female, as I was not able to find male dancers of Russian origin during the short period of the fieldwork project. One of the eight dancers was Bulgarian. She provided relevant information on the general situation of dancers against the background of the cultural policy of Bulgaria's government. The seven other dancers were of Russian origin. Two of them I could only meet once, because of their tight time schedules, so concerning most topics the unit of investigation consists of five persons.

As it turned out very soon, I had to redefine the terms *Russian dancer* and *Russian community in Sofia*, as these two groups did not seem to exist in the way I had expected them to. Firstly, Russians in Sofia do not form a clearly defined, closed and corporate community. Some Russian immigrants or their descendants were very active in Russian institutions like the Russian Cultural Centre, but according to the historian mentioned above, this was a minority.

Secondly, some of the Russian-speaking dancers I spoke to did not consider themselves Russian at all. They often came from different countries of the former Soviet Union and were in some cases not ethnic Russians, but Jews, Armenians, Kazakhs, Ukrainians or other. Some were either not willing to tie themselves down to a certain ethnicity, or they considered themselves as Bulgarian. Still, I decided to include even those who do not call themselves Russian in my study and to sum them up in the term *Russian-speaking*. In this way the project was to include people from different countries of the former Soviet Union, as well as those who were born and brought up in Bulgaria as children of at least one migrant and were able to speak Russian. Thus, ethnic belonging turned out not to be very important in my research, whereas language skills were rather crucial.

Furthermore, it was not easy to define who was a *dancer* and who was not. Initially I had hoped to concentrate on ballet dancers, but I could only find three Russian-speaking ballet dancers, one of whom was not able to participate as an informant because of a case of death in her family. So I decided to rely on a wider definition of dance. Belly-, jazz- and modern dancers were part of my group of informants, since all of them had received a professional training in dance and their dancing activity provided at least a part of the income.

Age distribution	**%**	**Total (N)**
20-30	28,6	2
30-40	28,6	2
40-50	14,3	1
50-60	28,6	2
	100	**7**

Table 1: Age distribution among interviewed dancers

Table 1 shows the age of the dancers involved in my study. Except for persons younger than 20 years, I was able to talk to dancers of every relevant age group.

To examine the resources and different forms of capital used by the research group, I subdivided the main research topic into four subjects. The first one referred to the actors. Grand tour interviews were helpful in order to collect some information on the individuals' biographic background. The migratory situation of the actors or their parents was mainly mentioned in those interviews. As I expected the family background of a dancer to be significant for my research question, I had planned to conduct some genealogical interviews. The genealogical method was the most time-consuming one, so that I only was able to apply it once.

Social relations were my second main subject of interest. In interviews about personal social networks I applied a formal questionnaire based on a name generator (Lang, Schnegg 2002: 19 f.). I was especially interested in the ethnicity and the profession of the actors' contacts.

My third topic of investigation concerned dance as profession. To find out what my key informants were exactly doing during the day, I conducted four time-budget surveys. Further, I led interviews concerning the economic dimension of dance to find out how the actors used their artistic abilities for financial purposes, what kind of economic sources they had access to, and whether social networks would matter in this context.

The diaspora context was the last relevant category. I led grand tour interviews concerning the history of the Russian diaspora as well as the contemporary situation of Russian migrants or other Russian-speaking people in Sofia. I had also prepared a questionnaire dealing with the mentioned issues for an interview with the expert.

In the following I shall first present a brief historical outline of the Russian diaspora in Bulgaria and introduce the core research group in this context. The subsequent chapter examines in which ways ethnicity, a common origin from the former Soviet Union, the ability to speak Russian or other kinds of cultural knowledge accumulated in Russia, have affected the actors' professional lives.

The theoretical framework of my study is based on concepts of *ethnic resources*, as developed in a study on migrants' "creative economies" in Vienna (Gebesmair 2009), as well as on Bourdieu's concepts of different forms of capital (Bourdieu 1983). Against this background, I shall consider dance as a creative profession and as a *mobile form of capital*.

Finally, I shall discuss different aspects of insecurity, referring to the general economic situation in Bulgaria as well as to the nature of dance as profession in itself.

Russians in Bulgaria

In the Russian diaspora five major emigration streams can be distinguished. After a first period of emigration of religious minorities[4] from Russia's Tsardom before 1917, a sizable number of ethnic Russians emigrated between the two World Wars. About 1 500 000 so-called White émigrés left Russia (Weiss 2000: 31). One of their migration routes led from the South of Russia to the Balkan states, where they hoped to stay temporarily, waiting for the collapse of communism in Russia (Raymond, Jones 2000: 7 f.). Instead, when Bulgaria became a part of the Eastern block after World War II, descendants of White émigrés were subjected to discrimination. As a result, many changed their Russian names to Bulgarian ones in order to conceal their origins. I was told by several informants that it would be difficult to find descendants of the White émigrés in Bulgaria at the present time, because they either had managed to escape the country during socialism, or had been integrated completely into Bulgarian society, hiding their Russian origins nearly their whole lives[5].

A smaller wave of Russian emigrants left during World War II. They were mostly workers who refused to return to the Soviet Union after the end of the war or surviving veterans of the forces which had collaborated with Nazi Germany. They mainly immigrated to the U.S., Australia and Canada (Ioncev, Lebedeva, Nazarov, Okorokov 2001: 62 f.; 118 f.).

About 300 000 political dissidents and Jews emigrated or were expatriated between 1970 and 1985. They first and foremost left for Israel, Germany and Greece (Ioncev, Lebedeva, Nazarov, Okorokov 2001: 85; 127). The last wave of Russian emigration was set in motion

4 Religious reforms in the 17th century led to a secession of the "Old Believers" (старообрядцы), from the Russian Orthodox Church. As religious dissidents, many of them emigrated fleeing the central authority and some came across the Black Sea to settle in Bulgaria (Interview 3, Anton, 10.09.2010).

5 Interview 3, Anton, 10.09.2010; Interview 9, Tamara, 16.09.2010.

through *perestroika* in the mid-1980s (Ioncev, Lebedeva, Nazarov, Okorokov 2001: 132).

According to a census in 2001, there were 15 595 Russians living in Bulgaria, mostly in the urban centres Burgas, Varna, Plovdiv and Sofia[6]. All Russian-speaking migrants I talked to had come to the country in the course of the last period of emigration. A significant part consisted of Russian women who had immigrated into Bulgaria for family reasons. During socialist times, Bulgarian men were prevalently sent to the Soviet Union for studies, where many of them met their Russian wives with whom they returned to Bulgaria[7].

In this way, the Russian diaspora in Bulgaria is dominated by women and is therefore often referred to as a "female diaspora"[8]. These women were often quite active within Russian institutions in Bulgaria, whereas many children of mixed marriages did not carry on the Russian language, as they grew up in a Bulgarian environment. Additionally, after the fall of socialism, Russian was no longer taught at school as an obligatory subject. The children were learning English and French instead and often distanced themselves explicitly from their Russian roots[9]. This aspect was affirmed by all my informants. Nearly all members of the core research group were either Russian-speaking women who had migrated to Bulgaria because they were married to Bulgarian men, or they were children of such mixed marriages.

6 www.nsi.bg/Census/Ethnos.htm (accessed 26.03.2011).

7 Interview 6, Vladislav, 14.09.2010.

8 "женская диаспора" (Interview3, Anton, 10.09.2010 [translation: M.K.]).

9 Interview 3, Anton, 10.09.2010; Interview 6, Vladislav, 14.09.2010.

Migration or family background	%	Total (N)
Migrated for family reasons (married to Bulgarian)	43%	3
Migrated for other reasons	14%	1
Child of mixed-marriage (born in Bulgaria)	43%	3
	100%	7

Table 2: Migration or family background

"Being Russian" as a resource

As mentioned above, the majority of the Russian-speaking dancers claimed not to maintain any kind of relation with institutions of the Russian community in Sofia. The historian, whom I considered an expert in questions of the Russian diaspora, estimated that approximately only 10% of the Russian-speaking people living in Bulgaria still participate in activities of Russian diaspora institutions[10].

However, two of my key informants indeed made use of ethnic resources in different ways. To analyse the particular cases, I shall rely on theories of capital elaborated by Pierre Bourdieu. Capital can appear in economic, social, symbolic or cultural forms, all being mutually convertible (Bourdieu 1983: 195 ff.). As the economic agency of individuals is embedded in their social and cultural sphere, the other forms of capital can be transferred into economic resources (Giordano 2008: 37). Personal networks tend to play an important role in business because of their ability to provide access to relevant information, services, or material commodities. These potential resources made available by social networks are referred to as *social capital*. The amount of the individuals' social capital depends on the number of their ties as

10 Interview 6, Vladislav, 14.09.2010.

well as on the amount of different forms of capital possessed by their contacts (Gebesmair 2009: 157 ff.; Bourdieu 1983: 190 f.).

Belonging to an ethnic community can facilitate an individual's access to certain resources (Giordano 2008: 39; Gebesmair 2009: 159 ff.), which are referred to as *ethnic resources* (Gebesmair 2009: 162 f.).

Diaspora institutions can play a major role in providing access to different resources within a migrant group. Events organised by the Russian Cultural Centre in Sofia enable the migrants and other Russian-speaking people to meet each other and to establish social networks.

Dinara, one key informant, regularly attended events of the Russian-speaking community where she met an economically successful community member. Even though both actors were hardly acquainted with each other, Dinara got significant financial support from the community member.

For members of a diaspora, specific competences such as knowing the language of origin or being familiar with different sets of norms and values can become ethnic resources which form a significant part of their cultural capital (Bourdieu 1983: 185 f.; Gebesmair 2009: 160f.). Knowing the Russian language, for instance, can influence the individual's economic situation. My informant Vera, who apart from dancing worked occasionally as a singer too, performed half of the songs she sang during a concert in Russian. As she told me, her audience often consisted partly of Russians. Although she claimed that she was not maintaining intra-ethnic relations, her cultural capital could serve to enlarge her target group as a singer.

Dance as mobile capital

In his study "*The Rise of the Creative Class and how it's transforming Work, Leisure, Community and Everyday Life*" Richard Florida (2004) defines the "creative class" as a social category including *"(...) people in science and engineering, architecture and design, education, arts, music and entertainment, whose economic function is to create new ideas, new technology and/or new creative content"* (Florida 2004: 8). The "creative class" is "*primarily paid to create*" in opposite to the "working class" which is "*primarily paid to execute according to plan*" (Florida 2004: 8). Thus creativity can be viewed as an economic resource, inasmuch as the creative agents use it for economic purposes (Barber-Kersovan 2007: 13).

In the examined cases, dance as a creative occupation proved to be a resource particularly because it can be considered a "portable profession"[11] which enables the actors to be mobile. Some of my informants had moved away from their place of birth and from their families at a very young age to start their professional ballet training in Moscow or Leningrad. While working as dancers, temporary engagements abroad or in different cities in the country of residence were remarkably frequent among nearly all of my interview partners. Dance is indeed an occupation that does not depend on a certain place of residence, nor on other immobile commodities. This potential mobility is especially relevant in the case of diasporas. Four of the seven interviewed dancers had migrated to Bulgaria. Being a dancer offered them the possibility to find a job in their original profession without the need for further training. Some became members of Bulgarian dance companies, others worked as ballet teachers and one even founded her own dance school.

In comparison to other artistic activities, dance is generally non-verbal. Firstly, this is decisively important for guest performances abroad. One of my key informants, for instance, was temporarily engaged in a Greek company. Knowing the Greek language was not a necessary condition to perform in Greece, nor did her Greek audience need to know Russian, or Bulgarian to appreciate her performance (Wulff 1998: 37).
Secondly, the non-verbal aspect is crucial in a diaspora, since it is not necessary to know the language of the country of residence to find a job. Viktorija had worked as an actress before she came to Bulgaria. Her

11 Re the correlation between mobility and economic specialisation in the diaspora, see Nefissa Naguib's study (2009) of Armenian photographers and jewellers. http://web.mac.com/terje.stordalen/CoCult/Naguib.htmlhttp://web.mac.com/terje.stordalen/CoCult/Naguib.html (accessed 12.08.2011).

language skills in Bulgarian were not good enough to continue acting in Sofia. However, as she had received lessons in different dance styles during her study at the famous theatre academy GITIS in Moscow, she was able to start a new career as a dancer. This also triggered her interest in pantomime. She began to take lessons in this explicitly non-verbal art and is now teaching it herself. The non-verbal character of dance is thus an important resource, increasing the potentials of dance as mobile capital

The Sofia Opera (photo: M .Kern)

Howard S. Becker's concept of "Art Worlds" (Becker: 1984) may serve to illustrate why artistic professions have such a high potential as mobile capital. Becker points out that professional artists share the conventions of their art on a local, national or even international level. This enables them to cooperate (Becker 1984: 55, 321 f.; Wulff 1998: 37).

Ballet in particular is a highly specialised occupation with an international consensus on standards. The core technique of classical ballet is globally the same, regardless of slight differences in the execution of basic steps in national ballet styles. French terms are applied internationally for designating steps, poses, and spatial directions (Wulff 1998: 37). The existence of a "*shared technical language*" (Wulff 1998: 37) makes it easier for dancers to give lessons in a country of which they do not speak the native language. This is an important factor in migration. It enabled one of my key informants to teach ballet at a Bulgarian institution immediately after she came to Sofia.

During socialism, artistic mobility was encouraged between Bulgaria und the Soviet Union. As a key informant told me, at that time Russian ballet artists were frequently invited to Sofia Opera to put on performances. In this way, Bulgarian ballet became strongly influenced by the Russian classical school[12]. During my sojourn in Bulgaria, I was often told about educational cooperation between the Soviet Union and Bulgaria. Students were invited to study at universities in different cities of the Soviet Union and were supposed to go back to Bulgaria afterwards. It was this kind of exchange that gave Anna, child of a mixed marriage who was born in Bulgaria, the opportunity to study ballet in Leningrad. After her return to Bulgaria, she continued working with Russian ballet masters and famous Russian dancers. Due to her Russian ballet training, she was elected eventually by a former artistic director of the Bolshoi Ballet to dance the star role in a performance he was staging in Sofia. This incident elevated her to the status of prima ballerina. As Anna accentuates, her professional training in Russia strongly influenced her success in Sofia[13]. The high reputation of the school she attended, the Vaganova Ballet Academy, certainly played a role too. Two other key informants also assured me that their professional achievements were due to the highly qualified training they had received in Russia.

---

12 Interview 10, Anna, 17.09.2010.

13 Interview 10, Anna, 17.09.2010.

The significance of the family

The access to the prestigious institutions three of my informants were privileged to attend, was limited and certainly still is at present times. Agents of the respective schools were delegated to recruit talented children in auditions all over the territory of the former Soviet Union as well as in Bulgaria. The children were often very young, when a lifetime decision was made for them by choosing them for ballet studies in Moscow or Leningrad.

In most cases, it was the parents' decision that made my informants start taking dance lessons at a preschool age. Apart from dance, some of them also received singing and music lessons. It was because of the affinity towards the arts of at least one parent, that the children obtained an early artistic education, which had a lasting impact on their further careers.

The process of cultivation and education has been described by Bourdieu as the individual's accumulation of embodied cultural capital. In this regard the investment of time is crucial for the educational process (Bourdieu 1983: 186 f.). Additionally, Bourdieu indicated the role of the family for the transmission of cultural capital between the generations. Growing up in a highly educated family increases the chance that the child will obtain a good education too (Bourdieu 1983: 186; Bourdieu 1996: 22 f.).

This is a given aspect in all above mentioned cases: The cultural capital my interview partners had access to through their family backgrounds was quite elevated. Most of their family members were highly educated. They were mostly active in science, engineering and the artistic field (see Table 3) and would in such a way fit into Florida's definition of the "creative class" (Florida 2004: 8). In contrast to specific *ethnic* resources such as access to diaspora structures, a command of the Russian language or the specific reputation of Russian dance institutions, I consider this area of cultural capital rather a *social class resource* (Gebesmair 2009: 162 f.).

Informants' parents' professions	N=10
Performing artists	4
Engineering, Science	4
Humanities: academia and teaching	1
Military	1

Table 3: Professions of the informants' parents

Given that my informants were socialised during communism, the aspect of economic capital was probably not pivotal in their cases. As a key informant told me, dance and music lessons were very cheap for everyone at that time. The government paid the pedagogues and other charges of the schools. Additionally, training at the prestigious institutions was financed by the state, once the agents had chosen the talented children. According to a dance instructor, it was much easier for dancers and pedagogues during socialism than it is nowadays. As the system has changed, so has the situation of dancing schools. My informant mentioned that it was difficult for her to attract pupils when she opened her school. Parents were very displeased by the news that they had to pay far more for their child's dance lessons than before the transition, and many could not afford it. Hence, the economic situation of the parents is becoming significant, as a higher amount of money is necessary now for enabling their children to take dance lessons. Since the investment in a ballet education is costly in terms of both time and money, the economic situation of the family is an important factor for becoming a dancer in post-socialism.

Insecurity, diversity and friendship

Nearly all of my informants mentioned the cultural policy pursued by Bulgaria's government in the late 2000s. The cutting of subsidy schemes for cultural institutions led to the closing down of theatres and to increasing unemployment of artists. Most of my informants and their acquaintances were affected by these measures. They lost job opportunities because many performance projects could no longer be carried out due to lack of funding. As a consequence, many artists were experiencing financial problems and job uncertainty. In general, work in the creative sector is affected by high uncertainty as work patterns are often unstable and most creative workers are freelancers (Gebesmair 2009: 161).

Nearly all of my informants had to rely on several jobs, although there is a marked difference between those older dancers who were not performing anymore, and the younger ones. Normally ballet dancers retire in their early forties or even earlier, as ballet dancing is physically highly demanding. A dancer's body is for many years exposed to extraordinary stress and its decline puts an end to a ballet career (Wulff 1998: 85). This is the time when dancers leave the stage and start a new career as teachers or stage directors, as a key informant told me. All three informants between 40 and 60 years had taken on a "*second career*" as ballet instructors (Wulff 1998: 85) to cope with the problem of ageing.

However, three of the four dancers between 20 and 40 were also giving dance lessons to supplement their income, since they could not earn a living by dance performances alone. Hence combining several jobs was an economic strategy in the first place. Apart from teaching belly dance, one key informant gained money through singing performances and her work as an agent for other artists. A young modern dancer who accomplished her studies in Dance Theatre at the New Bulgarian University had to work full-time as a sales assistant at a bookshop besides giving dance lessons for children.

According to a Bulgarian ballet instructor, every ballet pedagogue she knew had to rely on diverse places of work in order to make a living. This was contradictory to my initial assumption that ballet could be a more stable field of work than modern dance styles, because it has a tradition in Bulgaria. Nevertheless in the example of Elena, a middle-aged ballet dancer, her engagement at a ballet company provided her with a certain feeling of security. She was on maternity leave when I talked to her, and was sure that she would have no difficulties in returning to the ballet company. Still, as she was additionally working as a freelance choreographer, she was also affected by financial cuttings of the government concerning smaller dancing projects.

Regardless of the fact that the investigated cases were all very different from each other it can be summarised that nearly every dancer had to rely on several economic sources which caused a diversity of job-related activities, mostly all within the creative sector. So due to the lack of job security, freelance performing artists need to increase their potential for work opportunities in as many ways as possible (Dobson 2010: 9).

According to her study concerning musicians, Dobson reveals "*the need to be sociable and liked by one's colleagues and peers in order to increase chances of offers of work, or simply to retain existing work*" (Dobson 2010: 9). The importance of personal contacts between co-workers mentioned here is equally crucial for other artistic professions. Besides the economic meaning of social capital, in the form of access to jobs through personal networks for instance, a psychosocial component shall be added at this point. In consideration of the above mentioned insecure situation of artists, friendship relations provide the individuals with feelings of stability and reliability (Gebesmair 2009: 161). The latter is essential in a field that highly depends on cooperation. Becker describes the production of art as a collective activity of a cooperative network (Becker 1984: 1ff.). Indeed, to stage a smaller dance performance an often long-term cooperation of at least the performing dancers and the choreographer is required.

In the examined cases, friendships often arose from professional cooperation. This was particularly true for the younger actors who did not have a family of their own. After a dance performance one key informant participated in, all dancers involved went out for a drink together and I was able to observe that most of them were very familiar with each other. In an interview my informant confirmed that most of her friends were dancers she was working with or had worked with in the past. Another dancer affirmed that she knew nearly all her friends from work, and that she was mostly interacting with colleagues because of lack of leisure time[14].

On the other hand, personal contacts and friendship between colleagues can provide additional work opportunities, as in the case of two informants of the age categories 40-50 and 50-60. The women met each other by coincidence. The fact that they both originated from Central Asia was a bonding element at first. Still, they were too preoccupied with their work to meet frequently. Finally, it was their profession that effected an interactive relation between them, as Dinara who owned a dance school asked her friend to instruct at her institution.

Close relationships among cooperating artists constitute a resource in certain cases. In a state of job insecurity, they can serve as a source for work opportunities. Further, as artists often need to cooperate with each other or even depend on each other on stage while performing together (Wulff 1998: 89), a feeling of trust and reliability is of great importance.

Conclusions

Approaching my fieldwork project with the objective of investigating Russian dancers within the context of the Russian diaspora in Sofia, in the initial phase it sometimes appeared to me that I was dealing with two fields that did not belong together. According to the Russian-speaking dancers, there seemed to be no common context. My informants were claiming not to maintain any relationships within the Russian diaspora. Even though some knew about Russian institutions such as the Russian Cultural Centre, they indeed did not seem to cooperate on any terms with their members. The only exception maintaining relations with some diaspora institutions was Dinara. She attended events organised by the Cultural Centre and used the networks of the Russian-speaking diaspora for economic purposes.

---

14 Re. interrelations between work and private life, see also the article by R. Kleinknecht in this volume.

Still, the fact that most of the Russian-speaking dancers did not act within the context of the Russian diaspora is probably due to the particular structure of the Russian diaspora in Bulgaria. As inter-ethnic relationships such as mixed marriages were very frequent, most informants were well integrated into Bulgarian society and had no problems of adaptation.

Dance as a mobile profession seemed to be a further factor that facilitated integration. The dancers who were first-generation immigrants had in most cases been able to continue working in their occupation even without good skills in the Bulgarian language, which reduced the need to rely on ethnic resources.

Furthermore, considering that creative artists tend to share the "conventions" of their art independent of national borders or ethnic belonging, cooperating with Bulgarian colleagues did not seem to pose a problem. For dancers, maintaining good relationships with co-workers is important, as their work highly depends on artistic cooperation. Thus, even though in the most cases resources were not mobilised in migrant networks, my informants had access to social capital through networks within the creative sector.

Even though ballet in Sofia was definitively not dominated by Russian dancers, having completed professional ballet training at a prestigious institution in Russia indeed was a resource in itself. This was especially the case during socialism when the Russian technique was predominant in Bulgarian ballet. Still, it was no matter of ethnicity, as Bulgarians likewise had the opportunity to attend the famous ballet institutions in Moscow or Leningrad. It was rather the parents' investment in their children's early artistic education and the family's social background, which were essential for the dancers' careers. The generally high education of the informants' parents was striking in the investigated cases. Thus the results of my study confirm the significance of *social class resources* and the transmission of cultural capital as elaborated in the cited literature.

I also argued that currently, dancers in Bulgaria are facing a situation of high insecurity. On the one hand, the post-transformation cultural policy of Bulgaria's government has been characterised by significant cuts. On the other hand, work patterns of artistic professions are unstable and fast-moving and permanent engagements are quite the exception. Close professional networks are a meaningful resource in such a situation because they can provide the individual with further work opportunities. Additionally, given that dance is a highly time-consuming profession, free time to spend with non-colleagues is very rare. This is especially true in the case of dancers performing on stage. Consequently, dancers tend to establish relations of friendship with co-workers and often spend their leisure time with them, particularly if they do not have family of their own. Thus I conclude that performing artists are more likely to maintain relationships with colleagues than intra-ethnic networks. After all, both cases can coincide, as one example of the study shows.

In the end, it was due to the combination of diverse kinds of resources, rather than to one certain strategy, that the investigated individuals were able to make a living as dancers in Sofia.

References

Barber-Kersovan, Alenka (2007) Creative Class, Creative Industries, Creative City. Ein musikpolitisches Paradigma. In: Helms, Dietrich, Thomas Phleps (ed.): Sound and the City. Populäre Musik im urbanen Kontext. Beiträge zur Popularmusikforschung 35. Bielefeld: transcript: 11-30.

Becker, Howard S. (1984) Art Worlds. Berkeley [etc.]: University of California Press.

Bourdieu, Pierre (1983) Ökonomisches Kapital, kulturelles Kapital, soziales Kapital. In: Reinhard Kreckel (ed.): Soziale Ungleichheiten. Göttingen: Soziale Welt, 2: 183-198.

— (1996) On the Family as a Realized Category. In: Theory, Culture and Society, 13, 3: 19-26.

Dobson, Melissa C. (2010) Insecurity, professional sociability, and alcohol: Young freelance musicians´ perspectives on work and life in the music profession. In: Psychology of Music, 39, 2: 240-260.

Florida, Richard (2004) The Rise of the Creative Class and how it's transforming Work, Leisure, Community, and Everyday Life. New York: Basic Books.

Gebesmair, Andreas (ed.) (2009) "Embedded Industries": Soziale und kulturelle Ressourcen migrantischer Kulturarbeit. In: Randzonen der Kreativwirtschaft. Türkische, chinesische und südasiatische Kulturunternehmungen in Wien. Berlin [etc.]: LIT, volume 4: 157-179.

— (ed.) (2009) Randzonen der Kreativwirtschaft. Türkische, chinesische und südasiatische Kulturunternehmungen in Wien. Berlin [etc.]: LIT, volume 4.

Giordano, Christian (2008) Sozialkapital aus sozialanthropologischer Sicht. Eine kritische Betrachtung. In: Roth, Klaus (ed.) Sozialkapital – Vertrauen – Rechtssicherheit: Postsozialistische Gesellschaften und die Europäische Union. Zürich (et al.): LIT, 33-52.

Ioncev, V.A., N.M. Lebedeva, M.V. Nazarov, A.V. Okorokov (ed.) (2001) Ëmigracija i repatriacija v Rossii. Moscow: Popeèitel'stvo o nuždach rossijskich repatriantov.

Kloostermann, Robert; Jan Rath (2001) Immigrant entrepreneurs in advanced economies: Mixed embeddedness further explored. In: Journal of Ethnic and Migration Studies, 27, 2: 189-201.

Lang, Hartmut; Michael Schnegg (2002) Netzwerkanalyse. Eine praxis-orientierte Einführung. Methoden der Ethnographie, 1. (http://www.methoden-der-ethnographie.de/heft1/Netzwerkanalyse.pdf [accessed: 20.11.2011, 11:01]).

Raymond, Boris, David R. Jones (2000) The Russian Diaspora 1917-1941. Lanham, Maryland, London: The Scarecrow Press.

Weiss, Claudia (2000) Das Russland zwischen den Zeilen. Die russische Emigrantenpresse im Frankreich der 1920er Jahre und ihre Bedeutung für die Genese der "Zarubezhnaja Rossija", München, Hamburg.

Wulff, Helena (1998) Ballet Across Borders. Career and Culture in the World of Dancers. Oxford, New York: Berg.

Managing social relations in a Bulgarian yoga group

Ivan Raduychev

We enter the school and turn right through the silent corridor on the ground floor. It is Tuesday evening, end of August, and children still enjoy their summer holiday far away from the classrooms. We walk down the stairs to the basement, make a left turn and enter the doorway of the gym. It is a large room with some fitness gear lined on the side and huge windows reaching from floor to ceiling. Although it is half under ground, the hall is filled with light and the air is fresh. The wooden floor is pleasantly cool under my bare feet and I relax for a while on my yoga mat before we begin the session. There are about thirty people around me, most of them women, coming directly from their workplace, chit chatting and changing clothes. Ani invites us to close our eyes, to relax our bodies in a comfortable sitting posture, concentrate on the spot between the eyebrows and to chant the sacred OM three times. We are now ready to start with the first set of exercises.

Ani Pavlova has been teaching Satyananda Yoga in Sofia for more than twenty years. She was initiated by her reverend Guru Swami Satyananda of Bihar, India, in 1990. She was later given the task to spread his teachings in Bulgaria. During the time of my research, she was holding six classes every week in the gyms of two Sofia public schools, which the group had rented for this purpose. Once a week, on Saturday afternoon, members of the group gathered in the group's own yoga centre in Krasna Polyana suburb for joined prayers and chanting, sharing food and beverages, and listening to the words of the Guru recorded on videotapes.

My interest in this particular group was due to my private practice of meditation and yoga. I have participated in a number of courses throughout Europe and during my travels in India, so I wanted to see how yoga and meditation are being taught and accepted in my home country. I was surprised to see so many people coming to the classes each day, and to encounter many women at the age of my mother.

Initially. my questions for the field research had been directed at the processes of personal transformation a yoga practitioner experiences as his or her involvement in yoga gradually deepens: transformation of worldview, behaviour patterns and social networks. I was interested in how these three strains are interconnected, and how personal yoga practice can eventually influence one's environment. During the course of research however, and for the purpose of this article, I put an additional focus on the significance of personal relationships among the yoga practitioners as a form of social capital.

After a brief discussion of research methods, I will introduce the yoga group's composition and structure. I will then investigate the concept of different forms of capital as defined by Bourdieu (1992), applying them to the research group. Finally I will try to show how some aspects of personal lifestyle (change of moral values, time management and distribution of material resources) are being influenced by the practice of yoga and how these changes modify the social environment of the practitioners.

In the field: data and research methods

In order to uncover patterns of transformation that might occur when an actor involves deeper into the yogic practice as taught by a spiritual guide, I used different research methods to elicit the necessary data. Since group members met several times during the week to practice together, participant observation could be applied. The observations facilitated a closer personal contact to core group members and provided information about the structure of the group and the interaction among its members. Detailed information about the yogic tradition, its teaching and practice could be gathered during the yoga classes.

Although the exercises taught in the classes were not very physically demanding, initially it was difficult for me to participate in more than three or four yoga lessons per week: sore muscles, strains, exhaustion and sometimes light headaches occurred as side effects of the practice. By the end of the third week however, I started visiting all six weekly classes and also the additional meetings on Saturday afternoon. I even decided to undergo a "cleansing procedure"[1] under the guidance of Sila[2] and Ani. This was not a very pleasant experience and caused stomach disorders for a couple of days, but definitely contributed to my acceptance in the group: I had proved that I was willing to face challenges and to go deeper in the practice. By the end of the research period my body was able to exercise the given Asanas and Pranayamas with a greater ease, I felt generally very well and my sleep was sound and my dreams were as intense as I have had them during personal meditation retreats in the past.

The high degree of fluctuation of participants and group members during the classes caused difficulties in establishing initial contacts. The group consisted mainly of female participants and I felt insecure to approach many of them in the beginning, which put another obstacle to communication. Additional difficulties arose due to the time management of the informants: most of them were working during the day and came to the yoga sessions at 6 p.m., many have families. Being available for an interview would have meant that they should either leave work an hour earlier (which actually did happen in two cases) or stay after classes, that means after 8.30 p.m. which I could not expect or demand.

After about two weeks the distance had been gradually overcome and the first interviews could take place. I conducted grand-tour and semi-structured interviews (Bernard 2011: 156-187) with six of the main actors to obtain information about the history of the group and about the main topics of my research interest. Many informal talks I had could not be

---

1 Shanka Prakshalana – a cleansing of the intestinal tract and stomach by removing all residual impurities. The practitioner drinks in less then an hour around 3 litres of warm salty water in small portions and applies a special set of exercises, by which the water is guided through the intestines and washes the whole tract.

2 All names except Ani's are fictional since my informants preferred to remain anonymous.

recorded, as most of the informants did not consent to this. These talks were summarized in field notes.

The attempts to apply more formal methods of research, such as pile sorting after free listing (Bernard 2011: 233f), mental maps or questionnaires on personal networks (Schnegg & Lang 2001) failed to provide the desired amount of information. The main cause was a lack of interest and involvement on the side of the informants and, on the other hand, my own hesitation to apply the methods repeatedly after initial failures. Still, the acquired information gave me at least some insights on certain topics of interest: the adoption of foreign words, mainly of Sanskrit origin, into the vocabulary of group members (free lists and pile-sorting); places of significance in the context of the yoga group (mental maps); and personal relationships between group members (questionnaire on personal networks).

Demographical data, most of which as "second-hand information" (e.g. not directly obtained from each informant) was collected for 40 people who were involved in different group activities (Table 1). Out of these 40, five will not be taken into consideration in the analysis: three girls under the age of seven were brought to group meetings by their mothers; two young men aged 17 and 23 were only mentioned in an interview by their father for having taken part in group activities at some point in the past. Still, those five represent an important example of "socializing a second generation" into group structures and practices (Coney 1999: 145-168; Hardman 2004: 390-398).

	Male	Female	Total
28-34	1	8	9
35-44	2	4	6
45-49	1	6	7
50-59	4	4	8
over 60	2	3	5
Total	10	25	35

Table 1: Gender and Age distribution

As can be seen in the table, my female informants outnumber males by 2,5. This ratio was also very obvious during the yoga classes and meetings, where only between 1/5 and 1/3 of the participants consisted of men. On some occasions this relation dropped even further down to 1:8, but such cases were rather exceptional. The numbers shown in the above table are slightly higher than the total in benefit of the males for two reasons. On the one hand, being a male observer made my contacts to male informants easier, although not more intense. On the other hand, male newcomers (or male members I hadn't previously met) were so rare that I could spot a new male participant more easily than a new female one.

In the age groups "over 50" and "over 60", gender ratios did not show such high differences. One reason could be that there were not many people over 60 in the group anyway and some of them have already been practicing for a number of years (Ani, Emo, Todor, see also Table 3 below). In the earlier years, yoga groups were predominantly filled with male participants (interview with Ani from 07.09., Interview with Kaloyan from 27.09.) and some of them are still practicing. This is why, although new female participants aged 50 and older join the group, their number equals that of males in the same age category. Another reason is that persons over 50 are less involved in family raising issues than younger ones, so both women and men could take part in the classes. A third reason may lie in the essence of the yoga classes itself: Ani constantly underlines the health benefits a person can obtain by practicing yoga, especially concerning diseases usually attributed to growing age (irregularities of blood pressure, indigestion or lack of appetite, psychic stress, menopause or general lack of vitality). In comparison to other Yoga schools, the set of exercises given in these classes provides less physical challenges to people over 50.

At the end of the six weeks period I had gathered a total of 33 participant observation protocols and many additional field notes. I conducted six formal interviews, many informal talks and audio recorded two group sessions with chanting and prayers and two yoga classes. I took over 30 photographs and short videos and received around 20 pictures per email from a group member but was asked not to publish visual materials. After leaving the field, I sent per email questionnaires on personal networks and received two of them back, not completely filled in, but further information was denied for time and privacy reasons. I managed to apply free listing in four cases and two of the informants provided pile sorts of relevant concepts. In addition, I collected three mental maps which provided only limited information, however.

Composition and Structure of the Yoga Group

Depending on the locality where the group meets, there are between 25 and 60 people present at Ani Pavlova´s classes. Around 20 to 40 persons come to the group meetings in their own Yoga centre SitaRam on Saturday afternoon.

There are different reasons why people decide to join the yoga group. All my informants agreed that most participants attend the classes for health reasons, or in order to fill their leisure time with a meaningful experience. Another large part of the practitioners come because a friend or family member attends the classes and they feel like sharing a common activity. Only a small amount of people join the group in search of a spiritual path and not all of them decide to stay and practice under the guidance of Ani.

Most of my informants assured me that there is not a fixed network of people who compose the yoga group. Still it was obvious to me that some actors take a more active part in the group dynamics as others. The totality of participants could be roughly divided into three layers, arranged in the form of concentric circles (Fig. 1). Upon personal observations and based on the interviews, I could distinguish certain attributes that characterize the members of the different circles. These attributes are based on the degree of involvement a person shows in his attitude towards the group, its goals and its members. The presence or absence of some of the attributes is not compulsory for assigning a person to one of the layers but the probability is very high.

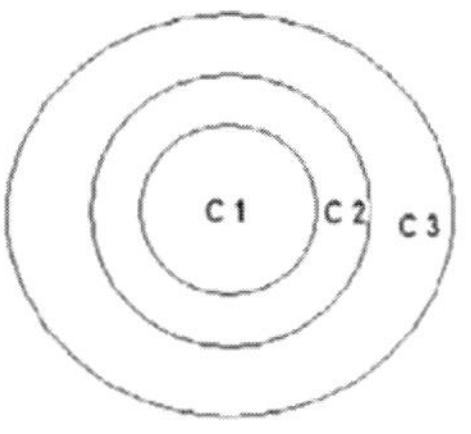

Fig. 1: Layers of involvement presented as concentric circles of participants

C 1: Ani is the centre of the group. She started teaching Satyananda Yoga in the 1990s and has been holding classes since the very beginning. Together with her, another about 25-35 people build the solid core of the group. Although there has always been fluctuation of people in this circle, the number of core members has remained quite constant over the last years (interview with Ani from 07.09., interview with Kaloyan from 27.09.). People belonging to this first circle attend diverse group meetings frequently (at least 2-3 times a week), and/or are taking part in group activities already for a number of years (at least four years). Another feature of core members might be their engagement in voluntary work for the benefit of the group and/ or financial support through monetary donations. Many of the core members have joined the group on several journeys to the mother Ashram[3] in India. They have shown a sincere interest and dedication to the teaching and practice of the group and have proven their reliability when needed. Whatever their motivation to join the group might have initially been, all of the core members have in the course of time acknowledged yoga to be their personal path of spiritual development. Most of them have been initiated by their Guru[4].

C 2: This layer consists of people who occasionally attend yoga classes or events organized by the group, but usually do not personally engage with the preparation of such activities. Most of the members assigned to the second layer do not consider yoga to be such an important part of their lives as people from the core group do. Still, some have travelled with Ani and/ or other members of the core group to the Indian ashram. Some have even undergone the ritual of initiation and have accepted the Guru as their spiritual leader. It is difficult to name the exact numbers in this layer but it could be estimated to around 100-120 people and tendency towards growing.

C 3: The wider periphery consists of people who only seldom attend group activities: once in a month or less, mostly only the yoga classes. Many of them accompany friends or relatives who participate in the classes. Their number should easily reach over 300 in the course of a year. If I am to estimate the number of people who have ever partaken in activities of the yoga group it should be well over 3000, excluding the large events when hundreds of people gather to meet a yoga teacher from abroad.

---

3 Ashram is a spiritual centre where a yoga Guru (very advanced spiritual master) resides and his followers can live, work and practice yoga and meditation. In the case of this yoga group, the ashram is situated near the village of Mungeer in the state of Bihar, India.

4 A person can be initiated by the Guru by accepting his guidance and protection. As a part of the ritual the initiated person also receives his own spiritual name and a personal Mantra (a specific verbal formula with a sacred meaning).

Age/ Layer	C 1	C 2	C 3	Total
28-35	8,4% (3)	11,2%(4)	5,6% (2)	25,2% (9)
36-44	2,8% (1)	5,6% (2)	8,4% (3)	16,8% (6)
45-49	5,6% (2)	11,2%(4)	2,8% (1)	19,6% (7)
50-59	5,6% (2)	8,4%(3)	8,4% (3)	23,4% (8)
over 60	5,6% (2)	5,6% (2)	2,8% (1)	15% (5)
Total	29% (10)	43% (16)	28% (9)	100% (35)

Table 2: Age of group members and degree of involvement in percent (absolute value in brackets)

Table 2 shows the age of the members of my sample according to their degree of involvement. In a total of 35 persons only 9 (over 25 %) are under the age of 35. Almost 40 % of the people are over 50. This distribution shows that only around one third (36 %) of the participants belong to the age group between 35 and 50, which is usually associated with high a degree of dedication to family and professional life. Out of the 10 core members, only 30% belong to this age group.

A possible explanation for the fact that younger and elder people devote time and resources to the group could be, besides a less time consuming profession and family life, a vivid interest in yoga. Many of my informants said, citing the yogic scriptures, that the best time to start yoga is in young age, so that a person can mature in the technique during adolescence and dedicate one's old age to the perfection and accomplishment of the yogic lifestyle (Interviews with Ani, Kaloyan, Metta, Sila and informal talks).

Gender/ Layer	C1	C2	C3	Total
Male	8,4% (3)	8,4% (3)	11,2% (4)	29% (10)
Female	19,6% (7)	37,4% (13)	14% (5)	71% (25)
Total	29% (10)	45,8% (16)	25,2% (9)	100%(35)

Table 3: Gender and degree of involvement

Table 3 shows an obvious predominance of female participants in the two inner layers of the group (C1 and C2). Only one of the male members from the C1 and C2 layers is younger than 48. Metta suggested (Interview from 29.09) that young males (age 20-35) might find the group less attractive for the lack of challenging exercises and the large amount of female participants aged over 45. Her previous spiritual experience has led her to similar groups where male participation is significantly higher.

Tables 2 and 3 show the total distribution of people I had contact with throughout the different layers of the group. The numbers given are disproportionate to the estimated size of the layers: C1 is estimated to consist of 25-35 people and I had contact with around 35 % of them. I had access to 16 out of estimated 120 members of the second layer – 13% and only 9 from hundreds of the members of the third circle. Since people of the last two layers attend the meetings less regularly, the contact with them was more difficult to establish. Also networks and connections between group members are strongest in the core group and lose intensity as the actors involved move to the periphery. Those actors from the outer layers, who wish to socialize in the group and become more active, consequently try to establish connections to people from the inner circles. Ties between actors from the third layer should be very weak, if existent, since the members have but little chance to occasionally meet during yoga classes.

Group dynamics

The boundaries of these circles however are not rigid but flexible. Persons can shift from one layer to another, depending on the intensity of their involvement within the group and their interest in yoga.

I shall illustrate this process on the example of Paritta (Interview with Paritta from 16.09.) which I believe could be generalized for anyone who would devote the necessary amount of time, interest and efforts to the practice taught in the group. The starting point of her contact with the group is shown in figure 2.

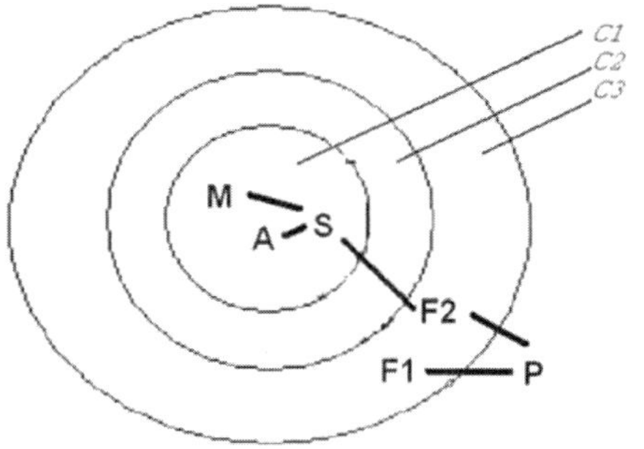

Fig.2: Initial contact with the group

Paritta's (P) initial contact with the group was provided by two close friends (F1 and F2) who have occasionally participated in Ani's yoga classes. One of them (F2) knew Sila (S) so she could connect Paritta and Sila after one of the yoga classes. Through Sila Paritta could better connect to Ani (A) and Metta (M). Being in touch with these key actors, Paritta could easily connect also with other (core) group members. Thus, using connections to people from the outermost circle C3, Paritta connected to the core circle C1 in very short time.

Her regular participation and involvement in group activities (both yoga classes and other meetings), her openness towards the practice and philosophy of the teaching, and her consequent visit in the Indian Ashram changed her position in the group in quite a short time.

Less than three years after her initial contact with the group, Paritta was a part of the core and was occasionally taking over responsibilities like shopping for the weekly meetings and helping to organize them. She knew a lot of the members from the C1 and C2 layers at that time (Kaloyan, Lidia, Todor) and became herself a link for outsiders to the group (F3). At the same time only one of the friends who initially connected her to the group remained in the group but did not change her status, while the other friend stopped visiting the sessions.

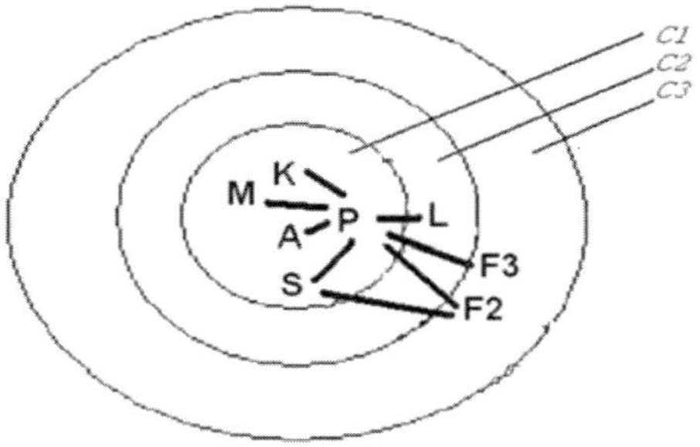

Fig. 3: Becoming a core member

However, after some time a conflict arose and Paritta felt insecure in her communication with some of the group members. She also had to invest more time in her new job and could not participate in group activities as often as before. At present, 6 years after her first contact with the group, Paritta is only rarely attending yoga sessions or group meetings. In terms of the figures above, we could say she changed her status from being an outsider to the group to becoming a core member and then shifting to the periphery again (C3 layer).

The example above shows the importance of personal relationships in Bulgaria, which does not apply only to family members (Barova 2008) or within diasporas (Kokot 2009), nor exclusively to their capacity for material rewards (Petrova 2008; Benovska-Sabkova 2004) but also to the structures of leisure groups (Benovska-Sabkova 2006). Each actor is connected to other members in different ways: more or less intense, in their roles as friends, relatives or acquaintances. Thus every group member has a unique pattern of social bonds and can use them in various ways.

Forms of capital and their applications for the group

The amount of actual and potential social relationships a person has accumulated in his network can be analyzed as social capital (Bourdieu 1992: 62). Through this network a person can get access to resources, be these material or other. Thus, social capital can also be transformed into economic capital (Bourdieu 1992: 65), provided social relationships were established and maintained for a long enough period of time.

The amount of social capital possessed by a person can largely determine the scope and range of his actions. This is true especially for countries of the former communist block where personal networks have always had vital importance (Petrova 2008: 128ff; Benovska-Sabkova 2004; Giordano 2010). This fact relates directly to the low level of trust towards institutions that is predominant in such societies (Giordano, 2006: 49).

Socialism, social capital and yoga practice

In the case of yoga practitioners in Bulgaria, the interrelations of social capital and trust have been vividly tangible since socialist times. The Bulgarian Communist Party was intolerant against religious activities, and since yoga has an obvious religious background, it was not allowed to practice it freely. The few yoga clubs in the country were subject to Party control and only the physical aspects of yoga were taught. In the 1960s, when Ani Pavlova started her personal practice with a Bulgarian teacher, she was meeting secretly with a group of others, who also showed a deeper interest in yogic spirituality (Interview with Ani from

07.09.). For this group, mutual trust was essential as opposed to the mistrust against Party functionaries.

"To practice yoga during socialism was as if you would walk the streets with a clockwork bomb in your pocket. If they got you, you could lose your job and your kids would not get admission in the university"[5]

Ani was herself taken to the police station on several occasions where she was interrogated and had to promise she would not practice yoga any more. Nevertheless, she and many others carried on their practice in secret, sharing only with trusted people (Interview with Ani from 07.09., Interview with Kaloyan from 27.09.).

A well-developed network of social relations did not only provide protection in times of danger (e.g. via ties to higher party leaders), but also gave access to material of spiritual interest. It was mostly through friends and relatives who travelled abroad, that yogic scriptures could be smuggled into Bulgaria and reach the yoga students (Interview with Ani from 07.09., Interview with Kaloyan from 27.09.). Finding a suitable place to practice and organising regular meetings also demanded good coordination among members and access to resources. Today, as the group grows and activities become more complex (organizing daily classes but also large international events) and more costly, social capital has not lost its significance.

Social capital and principles of reciprocity

Social capital is built on the principles of reciprocity, which may be direct (you help me and I help you) or indirect (you help me, I help him and he helps you) as well as immediate (fixed on a short term return of favours) or generalized (based on expectations of return in the future). Violating the principles of reciprocity can lead to the exclusion of an uncooperative group member, or in extreme cases, to disintegration of the whole group.

Although the yoga group is sustained solely by the voluntary work and donations of its members, reciprocity is not imposed as a compulsory principle of interaction, but taught as a moral norm. The readiness and

5 Interview with Ani Pavlova in the magazine Spisanie Edno, 77/2009: 79

ability of yoga students to give "selfless service without expecting anything in return" is considered an issue of personal development in the course of spiritual growth (Interview with Metta from 29.09., Interview with Sila from 12.09., Interview with Kaloyan from 27.09.).

Ani is the person with the highest amount of social capital within the boundaries of the yoga group. Her charisma and the way she communicates with others have helped her build a reliable network over the years of practice and teaching. Her contacts made large events possible[6] and eventually provided the group with their own yoga centre[7]. The personal connections to her as a teacher are very valuable for the group members: they can contact her on issues concerning their spiritual practice, health and personal issues, or at times even ask her for favours that require her to activate her own personal network and draw on its resources. Ani is the main connector to the Guru and the Indian mother ashram, as well as to other yoga groups of the same spiritual tradition in Bulgaria. She can thus recommend people and help them get admission in the ashram or on courses organised elsewhere.

However, Ani´s most valuable resource is her cultural capital: her knowledge regarding yoga and her involvement in the activities of the group. Decades of committed yoga practice and studies of scriptures have been necessary for Ani to accumulate this resource. Her own kind of "selfless service" is teaching classes six days a week, guiding the group during prayer and chanting meetings, and conducting rituals on particular

6 Swami Niranjananda, the present principle Guru of the tradition, visited Sofia in May 2008. He gave lectures on yoga and initiated followers in his spiritual tradition. A large amount of money was necessary to organize this event (over 2000 people participated altogether), most of which was donated by people close to Ani. In June 2011 Swami Satyasangananda, another important Guru, visited Bulgaria in a similarly large and costly event.

7 After holding their Saturday meetings (chanting and prayers) in not very comfortable locations for years, in 2008 a generous core group member bought a nice and spacious flat and donated it to the yoga group to use for meetings. Swami Niranjananda blessed the new place with his presence during his stay in Sofia.

occasions (e.g. Fire ceremony or Navaratri – an important Hindu holiday).

Fire ceremony in the Yoga Group (photo: I. Raduychev)

In return, Ani has easy access to support by other group members. Examples of her use of the social resources provided by the group can be taken from issues discussed during yoga classes. On several occasions, Ani mentioned that she needs assistance to find a new location where classes could be held. She asked the assembled group if anyone has personal connections to teachers or headmasters of schools in the central parts of Sofia. In a smaller group (mostly core group members) Ani mentioned that she needs help in personal matters. She does not explicitly ask for support, but rather describes a problem situation she is in and almost immediately receives offers to help from the group members present.

During my observations I noticed other group members giving and receiving help mainly in minor issues which demand less time and resources: writing a letter in English to the ashram, using someone's car for a while or sharing a ride, borrowing diverse items, etc. Since ties are denser between core group members, also the exchange networks are stronger there.

Captial and social resources

Ani's status in the group is also largely based on the amount of symbolic capital that has been ascribed to her. Being one of the most experienced yoga teachers in Sofia and in Bulgaria, Ani is highly praised by former students who have later become yoga teachers themselves[8]. Ani was interviewed several times in different mass media, for example during TV broadcasts on *BTV*[9], or in the magazines *Edno*[10] and *Eva*[11]. She is also known to be the private yoga instructor of the famous Bulgarian pop singer Yordanka Hristova[12]. Ani's symbolic capital is enlarged by her own actions as well: her appearance and behaviour are modest and sometimes mysterious, just in the way yoga students would expect an ideal yoga teacher to be. She reveals the secrets of yoga that have been given to her by her Guru, but does that step by step: "*The deepest layers of this knowledge*" - Ani says often during yoga classes – "*I cannot tell you, you wouldn't understand*". This underlines her exclusive place in the group in her function as "keeper and transmitter of wisdom"[13].

---

8 Some present Bulgarian yoga teachers are proud to list Ani Pavlova's name among their own teachers. Here some examples: http://www.yogainside.info/yoga_instructors_sofia.html; http://www.kiko-yoga.eu/?p=1; http://www.yoga108.info/sm.html; http://www.ambastyle.com/contact.html; http://www.yoga-bf.com/page1.html, etc.

9 http://www.btv.bg/news/story/139974

10 http://zine.edno.bg/showissue.php?issueid=77

11 http://old.eva.bg/index.php?option=com_content&task=view&id=4170&Itemid=7

12 http://www.bgestrada.com/bgestrada/?q=content

13 Ani's own spiritual name, by which she is known to many of the practitioners, is Shruti Gyana – "Keeper of the Wisdom"

In the case of the yoga group, the relations between cultural, symbolic and social capital are based on mutual dependence. The members holding the highest amount of social capital (Ani, Sila, Metta), also have a large amount of embodied cultural capital concerning yoga. They have good opportunities to display their knowledge in the communication with other members from different layers of the group. This inevitably increases their amount of symbolic capital since they are regarded by most group members as highly experienced and learned yoga practitioners that deserve respect and admiration for their dedication to the teaching. The growing symbolic capital in return makes them appear a desired person to connect to and a trustworthy fellow practitioner, which closes the cycle by increasing their social capital.

The use of social capital can provide actors with desired items, be these certain information, psychological support, help in problem solving or, in a few cases, material advantages. Reciprocity is not demanded as a return of a favour but expected per definition from any sincere yoga adept. In this context, voluntary work and mutual support are seen rather as a matter of personal development than as a result of social expectations. Since the topic of personal realization takes such a central place in the yoga practice of core group members, special attention will now be given to moral norms and their application.

Transformation of moral attitudes

A complete study on personal transformation following prolonged periods of intense spiritual practice would have to go far beyond the scope of the present six-week research. Still, my own experience with meditation and the personal stories of my informants as well as many personal accounts on the book market, support the thesis that practitioners undergo a positive change in life both on the physical and mental level[14].

14 Recent psychological and neurological research has even shown physiological change in the brain of meditation and yoga masters, as well as strong difference of emotional reactions to various stimuli when compared to non-practitioners (Lutz et

All my informants share the same notion of yoga: its teachings are based on certain moral concepts and its essence consists of deep spiritual practices that reach far beyond mere body exercises. Nevertheless, most of the participants (especially from the layers C3 and C2) practice the yoga exercises during the regular classes, but pick only certain aspects of the teaching that appeal to them and leave others aside. They find in yoga a meaningful and interesting addition to their daily routine but do not intend to develop the "yogic lifestyle" to the full. Compared to them, others (mainly from the C1 and C2 layers) decide to undertake a major change in their lifestyle so they can derive maximal benefits from their yoga practice. The ultimate goal of yoga is the absolute union with the divine and for this both body and mind have to be properly trained and purified, as Ani, Kaloyan, Metta and Sila stated during the interviews.

The efforts to adopt this new lifestyle and its moral normative system lead to a tangible change in worldview, habits and daily routine, life goals and priorities, patterns of social interaction, personal networks, and in many cases to a new distribution of financial resources.

For most of my informants it has not been easy to take a new course of life, especially when still bound to their old environment: family and friends, a job, and an urban surrounding. On the one hand they have to create a place for the new ideas in their own minds, on the other hand they have to defend these acquisitions also in front of society (Borowik 1997: 21). While some of the core members of the group enjoy the support and understanding of their family members (Ani, Kaloyan and his wife, Metta, Todor, Den), others had to face criticism and opposition (Sila, Paritta, Nanda, Anta).

For Sila it is not that important any more how her family sees her decision to devote to yoga. A major part of her social relationships are concentrated within the boundaries of the yoga group. Metta, Nanda and Paritta speak about a change of actors in their social networks. Since some of the earlier common interests have disappeared (going out,

---

al. 2007: 497-549; or http://www.youtube.com/watch?v=_mud-L6b0nM&feature=related).

consuming alcohol or drugs, etc.), former friends associated with these activities also have become obsolete. Also, the unwillingness of friends or relatives to join the yoga practice and thus share a common experience could create a gap even in close relationships.

A lifestyle in line with yogic philosophy gains importance for core group members and they try to implement it in their everyday life. The more intense the spiritual need is felt, the higher the probability that an actor would invest time, financial resources and emotions in establishing new personal relationships.

Open questions

All my informants stated that only profound personal changes can guarantee long lasting transformations of society. According to their view, it is the individual that has to change first. As shown above, practicing the technique of yoga brings about changes in personal lifestyle. A topic of further research could be the implication of such personal changes for Bulgarian society in general. Although the process of introducing and spreading yoga in Bulgaria is a very young one, it has gained momentum and attracts more and more people. This phenomenon is indicated by the constantly increasing number of yoga schools and studios in Sofia and throughout the country. The number of translated and published books on yoga and more general spiritual literature on the Bulgarian market is growing, as well as the interest of various public media for the topic.

It would be interesting to test the thesis that people who dedicate time and efforts to an intense spiritual practice, also get involved in other forms of civic activities. For a number of the core members of the research group this involvement seems to be a fact: some of them are active members of environmental organisations, of voluntary projects for the support of disadvantaged people, or of other spiritual movements. Others are working on projects that aim to coordinate and foster the efforts of civil organisations and charity foundations. From the informal talks I had with many of the group members, it appeared to me that most of them have already partaken, or are willing to participate in voluntary projects in Bulgaria and abroad.

The difference of numbers between male and female participants also needs further explanation, which certainly cannot be delivered after such a short period of investigation. Maybe a general survey of public opinion could give clues as to how Bulgarian men view the involvement in initiatives similar to the research group and what stops them from taking part in it. A comparison with other spiritual groups with different teaching and practice also seems reasonable.

Summary and conclusions

During my field research I investigated social relationships among and modes of interaction between members of Ani Pavlova's Satyananda Yoga group in Sofia. Although group meetings are frequented by many different people and fluctuation of participants is high, there seems to be a solid core group, which maintains the activities. A layer of less strongly involved participants surrounds the core and a third layer of sporadic visitors is included to represent the full picture of actors in the group.

Social capital appeared to be an important resource in this particular group which depends exclusively on the voluntary work and financial support of its members. These findings support previous research concerning social capital in Bulgaria (Petrova 2008, Benovska-Sâbkova 2004 & 2006, Giordano 2010, Kokot 2009). In the yoga group, the amount of social capital of an actor correlates positively with the amount of cultural and symbolic capital. Exchange among actors in the group is not limited only to material goods in the form of economic relationships, but provides group members also with emotional support and valuable information. However, contrary to many other examples where reciprocity is required for the maintenance of a relationship between actors, the members of the yoga group view reciprocity as based on a moral worldview and the wish for mutual support.

The intense yoga practice has caused personal transformations in the case of many core group members. Their attitudes towards themselves, their life goals and towards society have changed and they report an increased physical and mental wellbeing. Consequently the social networks of the actors have changed as well: many of the personal relationships are now focused on members of the yoga group or people with similar spiritual interests. In this way, spiritual seekers connect and establish new social groups, which may start acting in society as well. It is a matter of further research to show how successful and sustainable such a transformation could be in the case of Bulgaria.

References

Barova, Vihra (2008) A Bulgarian Example of Exchange and Reciprocity in the Family. Max Planck Institute for Social Anthropology, Working Paper No. 102, Halle/ Saale.

Benovska-Sâbkova, Milena (2004) Social Networks, Coalitions, and Clientelism at Workplace in Bulgaria. In: Klaus Roth (Ed.), Arbeit im Sozialismus – Arbeit im Postsozialismus. Münster: 109-128.

Benovska-Sâbkova, Milena (2008) Leisure Time, Friendship Groups and Social Capital in Bulgaria. In: Klaus Roth (ed.), Sozialkapital - Vertrauen – Rechtssicherheit: postsozialistische Gesellschaften und die Europäische Union, Wien: 183-203.

Bernhard, H. Russell (2011) Research Methods in Anthropology, Plymouth.

Borowik, Irena (ed.) (1997) New religious phenomena in Central and Eastern Europe. Krakow.

Bourdieu, Pierre (1992) Ökonomisches, kulturelles und soziales Kapital. In: P. Bourdieu, Die verborgenen Mechanismen der Macht. Hamburg 1992: 49-75.

Coney, Judith (1999) Sahaja yoga : socializing processes in a South Asian new religious movement. Routledge Chapman & Hall.

Giordano, Christian (2008) Sozialkapital aus sozialanthropologischer Sicht. In: Klaus Roth (ed.), Sozialkapital - Vertrauen – Rechtssicherheit: postsozialistische Gesellschaften und die Europäische Union, Wien: 33-51.

— (2010) Why new agrarian capitalists are successful in Bulgaria: the relevance of personalized social networks and face to face trust relations. In EthnoScripts, Hamburg, Vol. 12 (2010), 1, S.15-33.

Hardman, Charlotte E. (2004) Children in New Religious Movements. In James R. Lewis, The Oxford Handbook of New Religious Movements, Oxford: 390-398.

Kokot, Waltraud (2009) Diaspora as a resource? Managing social capital in the Armenian community of Sofia, Bulgaria. In: Greiner, Clemens and Waltraud Kokot (eds.): Networks, Resources and Economic Action. Ethnographic Case Studies in Honor of Hartmut Lang. Berlin: 127-150.

Lutz, Antoine et al, (2007) Meditation and the Neuroscience of Consciousness: An Introduction, Accessible at:

http://www.transpersonlig.no/sbs/pdf/Dunne_Ch%2019%20Lutz%20Dunne%20Davidson-1.pdf (accessed: 19.09.2011).

Petrova, Ivanka (2008) Aufbau von sozialem Kapital im sozialistischen und postsozialistischem Betriebsumfeld. In: Klaus Roth (ed.), Sozialkapital - Vertrauen – Rechtssicherheit: postsozialistische Gesellschaften und die Europäische Union, Wien: 127-151.

Schnegg, Michael und Hartmut Lang (2001) Netzwerkanalyse. Eine praxisorientierte Einführung. Accessible at: http://www.methoden-der-ethnographie.de/hefte/hefte.html (19.09.2011).

The resources of a women's NGO in Sofia

Katharina Kunze

Before I came to Sofia, I had done a short field study in Jerusalem at a women's non-governmental organization (NGO), which had been working with high ambitions, although with very little support. Apart from my research questions, this raised my interest in the question why this organization had been struggling for existence for such a long time. To understand why a particular organization is lacking in success, it is essential to know what successful ones are doing, which resources they use, and how different factors are connected to their success. This interest resulted in my field study at Animus Association Foundation[1] in Sofia.

The choice to explore Animus Association Foundation (AAF) was partly coincidental. The city of Sofia offered a common framework for all participants of the research group who decided on their own topics within the field of urban anthropology.

I chose AAF because I wanted to learn more about women's NGOs. My minor subject is Gender Studies, because I have always been curious about the way gender roles are presented, consolidated or deconstructed. My attention was initially drawn to Animus by a fellow student who in the past had worked at their hotline for victims of domestic violence, and by reports about Animus winning a price in Germany for their outstanding achievements in the field of anti-trafficking work. Presently I consider AAF as a best practice example, since it has become the most influential and best-known NGO in Bulgaria supporting victims of domestic violence and trafficking.

There is no common definition of the term "NGO" and statistics vary widely. For the year 2007, estimates of the total number of NGOs worldwide vary between 3,050[2] and 7,628[3] up to even 53,000[4] – counting just international but no national, local, grassroots NGOs.

---

1 Fondazia Assoziazia Animus www.animusassociation/org

2 statista.de

Nonetheless, there are some common aspects in all attempts to define the term "NGO": An organized community is working together on a shared goal in order to achieve a better situation for marginalized subjects, minority groups or endangered places, trying to popularize their aim and gathering procedural and methodical knowledge. Nevertheless usually one aspect is left out of the definitions: the fact that operating successfully is essential for NGOs as it is for every long lasting organization.

So one common aspect in diverse definitions describes mainly an ability to headline one´s own topics, but what exactly is necessary to popularize a goal, work on it effectively, to gain support and attention and to build up an NGO that can operate long term, has not been evaluated satisfactorily yet. In my field research in Sofia, I focused on Animus Association in order to explore the resources a women's NGO in Bulgaria needs and applies in order to gain stability in their existence, sustainability in their projects and coherence in their programs. Those three factors are what I consider necessary in order to call a NGO "successful".

State of research

I use the term "resources" in the context of NGOs with reference to Bourdieu´s theory of different forms of capital, which can be transformed into each other (Bourdieu 1983). In this paper, I extend his notion from individual actors to NGOs as organizations, asking for the specific resources Animus uses today and how they are traded in order to benefit Animus' goals.

So far, various factors contributing to NOGs´ success have been investigated separately. In his study of public relations strategies of Swiss NGOs, Schärer (2000) considers foundations and donors as the most important allies. Joachim (2007) also mentions allies as strategic partners

---

3 Bundeszentrale für politische Bildung

4 insm Lexikon

who help the NGOs or their umbrella organizations to enhance the status of their programs in the agenda of international organizations. Janett (1997, 165f quoted at: Schärer 2000) sees heterogeneous networks as the most important factor for successful NGO work, while Khatib and Rachid (1994) presume that a drawback automatically results in civil society movements which could be institutionalized into NGOs. For Keck and Sikkink (1998, quoted at: Joachim 2007, 178) moral authority and issue-specific knowledge are essential to be recognized as an influential NGO. This shows that different authors consider different factors as most important for successful NGO work and this correlates usually with the author´s own specialization and field of interest. This led me to the question: is there a hierarchy of resources at the current state of development at Animus?

Animus Association Foundation defines itself as an NGO. Although some programs initiated by this organization would not have been possible without the help of volunteers and unpaid experts, all of their latest achievements were developed and realized by professionals and employees who make a livelihood out of supporting Animus and its goals.

In the current literature on NGOs there is very little differentiation between types of NGOs, their size, their impact and the duration of existence. If there are specifications at all, they usually aim at the field of activism like ecological, humanitarian, political or advisory issues. Referring to the changes which an NGO passes in its history, two points of view can be distinguished: a founder-centered "inspiration theory" (Valsan 1994) and a "movement theory" which sees civil society as the engine of development (Joachim 2007; Khalib, Rachid 1994). Both approaches propose four different stages in the development of NGOs:

	Inspiration Theory	**Movement Theory**
1) initial situation	hidden problems	obvious problems
2) first activism	inspirational individual	critical group
3) gaining influence	cooperation with powerful allies (persons and/or institutions)	organizing & professionalizing volunteers
4) final strategy	foundation of specialized NGO	networking with other NGOs

Table 1: Different stages in the development of NGOs

According the "inspirational theory", a charismatic founder and leader is essential. Departing from Weber's notion of "charisma" (Weber 1922), the inspirational character of the founders in this case results from a worldly source: their observation of social problems and their ability to see possibilities. They may be the first ones to act, but they are not the only ones who know the goal and the way of getting there. According to Vaslan, "inspiration" is the ability to activate a common interest, shared goals and a joined strategy among people who are about to become volunteers, co-workers or sponsors.

In contrast, the "movement theory" is based on a scenario in which a number of people is increasingly critical towards their situation and start activism on a personal level. If there are enough activists at the same period of time, a network of civil protest is founded. The amount of work done by this group rises, until it is necessary for the volunteers to organize and institutionalize themselves. Public attention and the approval of unaffected persons and organizations result in wider networks and pressure groups.

Both theories are applicable but not sufficient to describe the development of AAF. Also, the theories were developed around 1994 - at a time before social network media communication simplified the exchange of information, ideas and strategies.

To understand the use of modern media for donor activation and education of the public, the significance of personal networks, shared values and common goals, anthropological studies of NGOs must refer to other sub-disciplines as business anthropology, anthropology of virtual space, and related subjects. Most studies in these fields however refer to organizations which are closely connected to payment and monetary benefits.

In contrast, NGOs are non-profit, but "*unpersonalized associations of people*" (Moosmüller 2001). The type of organization closest to NGOs seem to be civil society movements. Not long ago, the type of organization we call NGO today was named PVO (private voluntary organization), while NGO described literally everything that was non-governmental and not primarily economic including museums, churches, and clubs etc. (King 1994: 17).

The term "women's NGO" is used for both: NGOs that support women as clients and NGOs that are run by women. In many Bulgarian cases, both criteria apply although they operate on very different levels: Animus and seventy-five other institutions in forty Bulgarian towns (www.animusassociation.org) work on issues of safety and well-being of women within their families and social networks, while other women's organizations fight against discrimination of women in business, or aim to enhance feminist discourses in the media (Deimel 1998). As Payer (2006: 40) notes, 29 NGOs in Bulgaria (in a total of 660) proclaim in their name to be active in women's interests, forming four networks and umbrella-organizations, but still not a single one uses the word "gender" in their name or descriptive sub-lines.

Women in Bulgaria: a short historical outline

The first women's NGOs in Bulgaria were founded in the 19th century. Even earlier, after the independence of Greece, Bulgarian merchants had taken over former Greek business ventures in the Ottoman empire, gaining wealth and coming in contact with ideas of enlightenment. Literacy was developed throughout the country and among both sexes quickly, schools were opened and women started to work as teachers, translators and authors (Roth 1987: 196f). The first women's club of Bulgaria was founded as early as 1857 promoting education and more independence for women. From this time on the media started to discuss women's issues and in 1871 the first magazine for women's subjects was published (Zotschew 1987: 248).

With the "National Rebirth" of Bulgaria, the position of women became even more important (Roth 1987). Women were seen as the "educators of the nation" and were highly respected in this role. In girls schools the book "About Glorious Women" in which Stanka Nikolica Spaso-Elenia published an article about Bulgarian women was frequently read. In 1901 universities were opened for women (Roth 1987), but the women's movement was restricted to a limited area of professions for an educated upper class. The public position of women remained attached to their role in family live.

After 1945, open universities were established to extend the possibilities to study. Although the urban population grew by 300% between 1945 and 1984, a third of Bulgaria´s population still lived in rural areas (Zotschew 1987: 249). Especially women made use of the offer to study at home. 80% of the female students of open universities in Bulgaria were employed, most of them were married and many of them were young mothers (Zotschew 1987: 252). Even though the household and the family were still considered as primary obligations for women, they were additionally responsible for gaining a good education and supporting the society. There were very few limits for women in the choice of profession, but there remained an ongoing discussion if it was right to open male domains to women (Ilieva 1973: 119f quoted at: Zotschew 1987: 251).

Salaries were usually not high enough to raise a family with one income only, so women had to work additionally to their obligation to home and family. In total, women formed the majority of the Bulgarian workforce with 52.6% resulting from the fact that more men chose professions that made it unavoidable to work abroad and the military service was not considered as "work" in this statistic (Zotschew 1987: 250). Out of the working women, 84.9% had children, even though there were more abortions than births around 1979 (Zotschew 1987: 253). Divorce rates also were very high, rising to 26.3% in the cities in 1983.

The phase of transition after 1989 brought economic difficulties especially in the sector of "typical" women's professions. At the same time, new alliances were established and women's organizations were founded. The "Democratic Women´s Union" took up their work in March 1990 by establishing a whole catalogue of responsibilities for Bulgarian women, which included being patriotic, nurturing and gentle, taking care of the family, as well as succeeding in a profession and doing good for society. Closely connected to the Bulgarian Socialist Party and its communist predecessors (Deimel 1998: 262f), this union was one of the two powerful women's organizations at the time of Animus´ foundation. The other one was the Bulgarian Women Union (БЖС), a revival of a women's organization from the turn of the century, which was reestablished in 1993 in order to fight communism and to strengthen democracy.

Both organizations´ ideals and gender constructs propose a strict division of male and female responsibilities and tend to demand more from Bulgarian women than they are willing to achieve for them. Women's rights, women's safety and the situation of women in their own homes were not on the agenda of these two organizations, and most of their activities did not address minorities, but only the members of these unions.

Women in Bulgaria: the present situation

To understand the structure and activities of AAF, it is essential to give a short introduction to the current situation of women in Bulgaria.

The WHO index for national accounts of well-being correlates significantly with the deficit of trust in state institutions. In both aspects, Bulgaria inhabits the second last place in the European comparison before Ukraine (GeoWissen 47 2011). After 1989, poverty and unemployment rates rose much higher in the female population than among men (Deimel 1998: 257). In socialism, many women had earned their livelihood in "typical women's professions" like midwife, nurse or day nanny. When public kindergartens had to close within the privatization process those jobs got lost (Deimel 1998: 135). Particularly for young girls, it is increasingly difficult to find employment. 62% of the women without income were younger than 30 in 1992 (Deimel 1998: 50). In a survey in Sofia and Plovdiv, 92.7% of employers named "professionalism and experience" the most important factor among their employees. Still, only 26.8% would consider a woman for a leading position. Perhaps this is why every seventh woman thought that "attractive looks" were most crucial to get a job. (Deimel 1998: 154).

Women are underrepresented in the parliament (10.83% in 1998, Deimel 1998: 188). 36.1% of the men consider politics as important in their lives, while only 20.5% of the women think so (Deimel 1998: 190). 89.5% of the Bulgarian women can not imagine to be active in politics and having impact on decisions (Deimel 1998: 257). Still, 10% of the Bulgarian women are active in some kind of NGO work and 14.2% are members of a union (Deimel 1998: 257). Only 54% of the women feel economically independent and 84.1% claim that they are unhappy with their income ("ZENI 1997" in: Deimel 1998: 257).

Not only the private sphere, but also public life is dominated by gendered expectations. Even one of the first women's organizations in post-socialistic Bulgaria determined in its founding speech: "*Bulgarian women are patriotic, philanthropic and gentle [they are fulfilled] with love for home and family and the willingness to sacrifice themselves for the sake of the children*" (Платформа на ДЗС, in Deimel 1998, 261 Translation: KK).

With the foundation of a family, women are expected to take care of the home, the children, the wider family and they have to manage the daily budget.

Domestic violence in Bulgaria

Even though there were 37 so-called women's organizations registered in 1994 (Deimel 1998: 265) the foundation of AAF filled a huge gap in Bulgarian Society, as this was the first organization to focus on the issue of domestic violence.

The general climate of acceptance towards domestic violence is reflected in the following quote of an elderly, highly educated woman who showed empathy for male violators in a discussion: "*Family is the place for emotions. That's why violence is there, too. If your feelings are hurt you tend to hurt other people. The stronger the feelings, the stronger the reaction. It's only natural*" (participant observation KK, 6.10.2010).

All sources dealing with domestic violence in Bulgaria refer directly or indirectly to information provided by Animus. The fact that there are no other evaluations or official data is disturbing and underlines the need for NGOs like Animus in Bulgaria.

Domestic violence is a significant problem in Bulgaria. Even teenage girls state that they are afraid to start relationships because they expect to be controlled, dominated and physically hurt by a boyfriend (Minnesota Advocates for Human Rights 1997). Abusing one´s partner is hardly punished by courts, except for an average 15 cases per year in Sofia alone in which quarrels between husband and wife result in her death. Other injuries are categorized as "strong", "medium" and "light" in the Article 263 of the Bulgarian penal code. "Strong" assault describes the permanent loss of one sense, ability to speak or fertility (Datcheva 2007: 111). "Medium" injuries are for example the loss of a sense on one side of the body only, broken bones or burnings that heal after some time. All other injuries are considered as "light", not included are feelings of threat, fear or insecurity. Legal punishment for violence within a partnership is usually very gentle – if there is a trial at all. 60% of the Bulgarian women either don't know about laws implemented to protect them and/or are unable to use this knowledge in case of emergency (Animus Workshop 7.10.2010). The laws against domestic violence were implemented in 2004 with the help of AAF, but there still are no legal instruments if a restriction order is not followed.

The high rate of cases of domestic violence – more than 2,000 women from Sofia alone seek help at AAF every year – endanger the women's future as well as their well-being: 98% of the Bulgarian victims of trafficking have experience with domestic violence (Interview Ani Torozova, Director of the Crisis Center of Animus, 7.9.2010) and many women are forced to stay in the violent household by their economic situation because there are no women's shelters in Bulgaria except from those maintained by Animus and a few other private organizations.

Social pressure also makes it difficult for women in Bulgaria to escape an endangering situation. There is a tendency to blame then women who escape from violent partners. The abuse is frequently justified with the argument that leaving her husband shows her unfaithfulness, which proves that he was right all the time to punish her in advance, which is seen as his right as a loving husband (Interview Eli 1.10.2010).

When AAF was founded in 1994, there was no public discourse about domestic violence in Bulgaria. The "Minnesota Advocates for Human Rights" explored domestic violence in Bulgaria by talking with hospital employees and NGOs and assumes that the reasons lie in an ideological equation of the family and the nation in Bulgaria. To admit that there is something essentially wrong within a huge number of Bulgarian families would result in admitting that there are problems within Bulgarian society.

Animus Association Foundation: aims and organizational structure

Animus Association is a part of "La Strada International", a "European network against trafficking in human beings with a focus on Central and Eastern Europe" (www.lastradainternational.org). As about 40 volunteers are supporting Animus´ work in the hotline for victims of domestic violence, it was not always easy to say where the organization begins and where it ends. By restricting my group of informants to the employees working in the same building, I was able to easily observe their interactions. However, the language barrier made it difficult for me to divide between private and business related talks. Still, participant observation led to important data about the quality of network connections, work processes, time management and hierarchy.

Fifteen women and one man are working constantly at AAF, another man (a former professor of the founders) participates in the supervision meetings. IT-support, cleaning personnel and a janitor were not included in my group of informants, because their work is not directly related to Animus' goals, although it certainly is valuable to Animus itself.

Room 1: The front desk of Animus Association Foundation. Whoever enters AAF comes here first. The phone is usually busy and the psychologists' office next door also contributes towards a lively atmosphere. (Photo: K. Kunze)

Animus was founded in 1994 by Maria and Nadejda, two psychologists working in hospitals, based on their experiences with treating children and their mothers. A former male professor of the founding directors offered his help and was willing to integrate this project into his activities, but they declined in order to stay independent from "patriarchal power structures" (Interview Nadejda 14.09.2010). This way AAF started the Crisis Center for victims of domestic violence in 1995. In the same year Nadja, a former co-student and psychotherapist, joined her friends and in 1996 another colleague took over PR work for Animus. The foundation grew and initiated more and more projects. Since 1998 AAF is a partner of the La Strada International network against trafficking and at the same time Animus started to organize, host and execute educational programs. The women working at Animus had become experts and were now teaching about anti-trafficking work, prevention and diagnosing of domestic violence, as well as NGO-founding in universities, congresses, police academies or in academic workshops. This spread their influence, improved their image and secured the financial basis for further projects because they were not relying on donations only, but earned their own money. In the year 1999 the training program of Animus was reorganized as a Training Center, offering courses and workshops in trauma therapy, community work and organizational consulting (www.wave-network.org). Those trainings have been held throughout Europe and can be booked in Bulgarian, English and Russian. More languages are possible on request.

Playroom, first floor: This room is equipped and used for children and family therapy. Whilst playing with the youngest, the psychologists of AAF identify family rituals, hidden structures and possibilities to change abusive or violent behaviour. (Photo: K. Kunze)

The project that AAF is most known for in Sofia is the hotline for victims of domestic violence, a 24 hour free-of-charge telephone service where women can find therapeutic help and practical advice. It was broadened into the Children Help Line with a European harmonized number and receives support from various Bulgarian companies: There are stickers in all the buses of Sofia advertising the number and inviting to call in difficult private situations. A telephone provider took over the costs of all calls for one year and there is state funding as well to secure the persistence of this project (AAF annual report 2009). Students volunteering for the telephone service can earn credit points for their studies and about 40 young women support this project by spending their free time as unpaid helpers at the moment.

In 2004, Animus moved to their current address into a building of their own, which was renovated and decorated by the staff.

The growing influence of Animus extends to the formulation of new laws against domestic violence or for the security and equality of women. Furthermore Animus filed a law suit against a Bulgarian brewery because of their sexist advertising, which gave them public attention and supported their image as an NGO committed to feminist causes.

In 2009, Animus started 18 new projects in the field of prevention of violence, family support and education of youth. They conducted 145 workshops and trainings for 1,370 participants in total and started a two semester alumni course for post-graduates. In the same year, 6,320 calls reached the hotline and 2,649 persons had to be transferred to the Crisis Center or for consultation (AAF annual report 2009).

Room 4 Couch: The psychologists with an individual office could chose their favourite furniture and interior design. This keeps the atmosphere very private since the psychologists show something of themselves - like paintings made by the husband. (Photo: K. Kunze)

Currently AAF tries to hand over established and well going projects to the state, because they create sizeable running expenses but do no longer need specific expertise.

Animus is also striving to make psychotherapy a subject at Bulgarian universities because up to now one can study psychology only. So far, the public image of psychotherapy is not very popular. I asked Bulgarian students under which conditions they would think about consulting a psychotherapist, and they all regarded this as a kind of last chance in cases of serious mental illness only. Everything less disturbing, such as depressions, burn-out syndrome or insecurity about one´s own decisions, would rather be discussed with family members or kept to oneself (Field notes, KK 22.09.2010).

Factors of success: hierarchies and strategic use of recourses

Based on the results of my field research, I will take a closer look at the resources AAF´s success is based on. I will explain which factors are crucial for its popularity in Bulgarian society, for the effectiveness of the projects and for the sustainability of the NGO´s programs.

As described earlier, the lack of women's NGOs at the time of transition had initiated the foundation of AAF. The high amount of women suffering from domestic violence in Bulgaria emphasized the importance of this NGO and increased its influence on political decisions and juristic phrasing. On the other hand, Animus´ work is still hindered by reservations in Bulgarian society against psychotherapy´, as well as by strong norms against discussing family conflicts in public.

In the following chapter I shall present a model of AAF´s use of resources and of the current state of its development. First, I will describe each of the five resources that my research has shown to be most important for AAF individually, within the framework of Bourdieu´s (1983) concepts of different forms of capital.

The *employees* share a specific understanding of their work that was unique at the time when Animus was founded. While the majority of the Bulgarians seem to consider psychotherapy as inappropriate and domestic violence as a minor issue, the employees of Animus are active to change this ideology. They work together on the same goals and differentiate themselves from other organizations. This seems to support the solidarity within their group and probably held their motivation on such a high level for many years.

The average employee[5] at Animus is a 36 year old woman working as a psychologist or psychotherapist, living with her husband and one child in their own flat. This average employee was 10.33 years older than her mother at the birth of her first child. She herself is her mother´s firstborn and her parents are still married and healthy. These parents are

5 These figures are based on a compilation of my field data.

highly educated and/or self employed. Moreover she was born in Sofia and worked in 1.75 jobs at NGOs or Hospitals that gave her some additional qualification for her current responsibilities before she came to Animus. At Animus, this average employee is responsible for 2.31 other things than psychotherapy, which mainly means project coordination.

The homogeneity among the group is a positive factor for solidarity, too. As Francis Fukuyama pointed out, societies with a low degree of trust in political institutions and official procedures, relate strongly to personal networks and similarity (Fukuyama 1995). As the WHO happiness index showed, Bulgaria is one of the lowest trusting countries in Europe. Therefore family, kinship and locality are very important for social stability. A similar life situation, shared moral beliefs and the same phase of life create an atmosphere that makes it easy to get to know each other, build up friendships, trust one another and therefore form a productive working environment.

Another essential factor within the resource "employees" is the high degree of education and qualification that all had earned before coming to Animus. All of them had gained relevant experience in other jobs and brought in specific talents and further interests to broaden Animus' portfolio. Work is nearly never delegated by the directors to someone within the team, but there are always helpful coworkers. No one seemed afraid to start new projects, to spend weekends at conferences or to do some extra work. At the weekly meetings, everyone reported their progresses and difficulties and as soon as someone needed help someone else volunteered and offered support.

To summarize, the employees form a significant resource for Animus´ success. Shared visions, homogeneity, qualification and independence are the factors that make it most important for Animus' development in the past and in the future. At the very beginning, there were no other resources than the will and the qualification of the founders, while today AAF is so well known that they received more than a dozen applications within one week when a position as an international expert was vacant. They can choose with whom to work. If someone is just qualified but does not become an accepted member of the team this person has to leave soon.

As the second most important resource, I have identified the *ideas and innovations* provided by AAF. To recognize the lack in official support systems and to realize a need for action was essential for the foundation of AAF. The founders have kept up this strategy of identifying problems and starting specific projects at this point until today. They encourage their employees to start their own projects, to travel to conferences and to be informed about political and social changes at all times. Also they are eager to give away established and well running projects to create the capacity for new ones.

Furthermore AAF is not only a center of support and consultation for women and children, it also holds a strong lobbying position as experts in the media and among political decision makers. Workshops, lectures and alumni spread their knowledge and their theoretical approach to the support of women.

Innovations and ideas are a resource which is also dependent on the choice of employees. Their ability to recognize possibilities and to come up with well fitting solutions is essential at this point. At the same time, an inspirational surrounding motivates the employees, helps against the boredom of routine and makes AAF a desired workplace for young professionals.

As I already emphasized when discussing the employees, strong *social ties* based on relations of friendship are very important for AAF´s success and for their ability to work at short notice and with high esprit for so many years. Not only the "senior employees" knew each other before they started working together, also other employees were hired on recommendation by mutual friends or acquaintances. This indicates a policy in which knowing each other personally may be the key point, if several applications with the same qualification are sent in.

But personal relations are not only used for the choice of employees, they are also very important for AAF beyond the organization: Nearly all of the current employees come from families that were well established and successful already during socialism. Most of them were born in Sofia, their parents had studied – some abroad – and held professions like engineer, artists or were working in the media. Growing up in such a surrounding can provide cultural as well as social capital. Not only do the parents know important members of society, one´s own friends and former schoolmates may become influential and powerful later on. Since the transition in Bulgaria was not very abrupt, a lot of structures were preserved. This heritage helped AAF a lot in the first years (Interview Katja 1.10.2010).

Later, when Animus had become a well known institution the resource of networking was more important on the professional level than in private space. Knowing other NGOs abroad made it possible to form La Strada. Being involved in the foundation of other NGOs encourages exchange of projects. This way the core of each organization can be specified in such a way that competition is reduced as much as possible. Keeping contact with other NGOs worldwide at conferences has a huge impact on the organization´s programs and innovations because it informs AAF about possible solutions and best practice examples from other places. The portfolio of Animus is considered unique in Bulgaria among the employees (Pile Sorts, KK) and if donors and foundations have the same impression this can influence the decision of granting money or not. While employees and ideas are essential resources for efficiency for the high amount of work executed, networking with other NGOs can be immediately transferred into economic capital, as I will show in the following passage.

Money is obviously a resource of major importance for any NGO. At the early phase of an NGO, a lot can be achieved with very little funding. In later stages however, salaries and rents for an office have to be paid and running programs need to be financed. Therefore, donors are important to enable the progress of NGO work. They are best convinced by qualified employees, good ideas and – of course – networking. Public and private donors can be approached by presenting ideas and interesting public relations work.

In the case of Animus, costs have been reduced by buying an own house instead of renting office space, and by organizing trainings and workshops to gain money. AAF uses its expertise and specific knowledge to be partly self-subsistent by selling their unique insights in lectures and trainings.

As outlined above, experience and strong relations of trust among the team which can only be built up in the course of time, have been most important for AAF´s success. The salaries of the employees seem to be adequate to generous, which is a factor of cost reduction in the long way, too: If employees are satisfied with their job situation, they are less likely to leave. In fact, I was told that most of the former employees who had left AAF, had done so because they emigrated or had founded their own NGOs. On one hand, this was a loss for Animus, but it had a positive impact on networking on the other.

With the challenges of NGO work and the experience gained at AAF, all co-workers have become highly qualified experts and competent project coordinators very quickly. These aspects could be used profitably in economy or in private clinics, where salaries usually are higher than in the non-profit sector. So giving a good payment to the employees, keeps them motivated and on the job for a long time and guarantees that they concentrate on new ideas and innovations.

It also helps that the psychologists and psychotherapists are allowed to do some private practice work in the organization´s office space. Regular paying patients come without a history of domestic violence and without a court order. This brings some "lighter" topics into the daily routine of the psychotherapists and also raises their salaries and the budget for upcoming projects.

Since the number and quality of projects an NGO can realize depends on the extent of money it is able to raise, the issue of clients is also closely connected to this factor.

The first *clients* of AAF were women suffering from physical abuse and domestic violence. Today, the range of clients also includes children who experience trouble at home, victims of trafficking, women who need psychotherapy, as well as families asking for advice (private patients turning to Animus shall be left out of my further discussion, since they are not dependent on the NGO-work). All original clients of Animus are victims, in a powerless position and facing problems everyone can relate to. Consequently, the willingness to help and support this type of clients is relatively high. Animus does not present itself as a feminist organization by women for women only, but as a guardian of "*healthy communication between people and gender equality in Bulgarian society*"[6]. By framing their goals in this motivational way, they raise moral support from a broad majority. "Motivational framing" refers to presenting a topic as prototypical for a general discourse, and to show thereby that a change in this one aspect can lead to improvements in many more areas (Joachim 2007). Since even strong supporters of traditional gender roles would not seriously vote for "unhealthy communication", AAF is morally protected and can rally support by a wide majority in Bulgarian society.

Focusing on clients who are publicly accepted as victims (instead of those who are perceived as having produced their own problems, such as drug-users or stigmatized minorities), puts their pain in a context that shows that helping them is helping society as a whole. This makes it easier for donors to support the NGO and nearly impossible for opponents to argue against their projects. The right category of clients can therefore be seen as a resource which can be almost directly traded for economic support.

6 www.animusassociation.org/en/mission-and-goals/

Conclusions

During my field study at AAF, I investigated the use of different resources and the conditions of success for a women's NGO in Bulgaria. Initially I had hoped for data that were transferable to other NGOs, but the situation of Animus Association Foundation is very specific. It was the first organization of its kind (which led to immediate funding and popularity) in a country with low trust towards official authorities in a time of massive political and social changes.

The combination of these factors created a popular, respected, and ambitious NGO. The founders, early co-workers and board members used their qualification, influence and knowledge to stabilize those first successes. Innovative ideas have led to a broad target market and turned volunteers and helpers into experts and lobbyists. Networks – private, political and professional – strengthened Animus´ unique position as a central actor within the NGO-landscape of Bulgaria and Eastern Europe. At this point, money was not a problem anymore. "Every proposal got granted" (Interview Nadja 17.09.2010), media and politics turned to Animus for their assessment (Interview Katja 1.10.2010) and finally even the costs of rent were abolished.

In summary, AAF can be seen as a best practice example for other NGOs, but also as an organization that was lucky to unite many positive resources.

So far, I have only concentrated on the internal organization and value structure. Apart from the question if and how far the results are transferable to other organizations, it would also be interesting to evaluate the image of AAF in Bulgaria among partners, population and politicians. A possible extension of this study also ought to investigate the use of resources by further successful NGOs. Based on these examples, recommendations to NGOs could be developed with regard to specific aspects of their work which may need to be supported or changed.

References

Bourdieu, Pierre (1983) Ökonomisches Kapital, kulturelles Kapital, soziales Kapital. In: Reinhard Kreckel (ed.): Soziale Ungleichheiten. Göttingen: Soziale Welt, 2: 183-198.

Datcheva, Dessislava (2007) Das bulgarische Straf- und Strafprozessrecht in kritischer Darstellung seiner Rezeptionsgesetze. Hamburg: Recht in Ostmittel- Südost- und Osteuropa/GUS, vol. 9.

Deimel, Johanna (1998) Bewegte Zeiten. Frauen in Bulgarien gestern und heute. In: Gumpel, Werner (ed.) Wirtschaft und Gesellschaft in Südosteuropa, vol. 13, München.

Fukuyama, Francis (1995) Trust. The Social Virtues and the Creation of Prosperity. New York.

Joachim, Jutta (2007) Agenda Setting the UN, and NGOs. Gender Violence and Reproductive Rights. Georgetown University Press.

El Khatib, M.F. and Rachid, A.R.H. (1994) NGOs in Egypt: A General survey In: Bonser, Ringeling (ed-): The Role of Non Governmental Organizations (NGOs) in national developement strategies in Arab and middle East countries. Bruxelles: 19-22.

King, Robert G. (1994) Toward a Classification of Organizations. In: Bonser, Ringeling (ed.): The Role of Non Governmental Organizations (NGOs) in National Developement Strategies in Arab and Middle East Countries. Bruxelles: 15-19.

Minnesota Advocates for Human Rights (1996) Domestic Violence in Bulgaria.

Moosmüller, Alois (2001) Interkulturelle Beratung und Organisationsentwicklung in multinationalen Unternehmen: Zwei Fallstudien. Vortrag am 16.02.2001 in Berlin bei der Tagung „Das Innenleben der Organisation. Ethnographisches Wissen in der Organisationsberatung".

(http://www.arbeitskulturen.de/down/07moosmueller.htm [retrieved 14.11.2011]).

Payer, Silvia (2006) Eastern European Women's organizations in times of EU enlargement. Wien.

Roth, Juliana (1987) Lehrerinnen, Übersetzerinnen, Literatinnen: Bulgarische Frauen im 19. Jahrhundert. In: Reiter, Norbert (Hrsg): Die Stellung der Frau auf dem Balkan. Beiträge zur Tagung vom 3.-5. September 1985 in Berlin. Wiesbaden: 193-201.

Schärer, Felipe (2000) Die Öffentlichkeitsarbeit der NGOs. Bern.

Valsan, E. L (1994) Role of Leadership in Non-Governmental Organisations In: Bonser, Ringeling (ed.): The Role of Non Governmental Organizations (NGOs) in National Developement Strategies in Arab and Middle East Countries. Bruxelles: 59-72.

Weber, Max (1922) Wirtschaft und Gesellschaft. Grundriss der verstehenden Soziologie. (http://www.textlog.de/weber_wirtschaft.html).

Zotschew, Theodor (1987) Stellung der Frau im heutigen wirtschaftlichen und gesellschaftlichen Leben Bulgariens In: Reiter, Norbert (Hrsg): Die Stellung der Frau auf dem Balkan. Berlin: 247-254.

Websites and Press Releases cited:

GEO Wissen 47, 5/2011 "Glück".

http://www.insm-lexikon.de/ngos---nicht-regierungsorganisationen.html (retrieved 17.06.2011).

www.lastradainternational.org (accessed: 17.06.2011)

http://de.statista.com/statistik/daten/studie/158268/umfrage/entwicklung-der-anzahl-von-ngos-weltweit-seit-1948/ (accessed: 17.06.2011).

http://www.wave-network.org/start.asp?ID=20770&b=151 (accessed: 17.06.20).

Evolving elements of civil society in Bulgaria: The example of environmental activism

Mira Carla Höpfner

Due to the current processes of integration within the European Union and the processes of democratization and modernization in South Eastern Europe, the issue of civil society has been of growing importance also in Bulgaria. Civil society plays an increasingly important role all over the world, but knowledge about the state of civil society is in many cases limited. This is also the case in Bulgaria and the main reason why I saw the need for further investigation and research into difficulties, perspectives and incentives for the development of civil society in Bulgaria today, especially in the spectrum of environmental activism.

This article evolved from data collected during a 6-week field excursion in Sofia and it is based on existing theories and findings concerning this topic. However, it must be mentioned that the general tenor of some articles is rather pessimistic and negative concerning the evolvement of a civil society in the post-communist transition countries and especially in Bulgaria.

In the following, I will present three viewpoints on the development of civil society in Bulgaria, as stated by Klaus Roth, Christian Giordano and in Francis Fukuyama's theory of *low trust/high trust societies* (Fukuyama 1995). I will work with the concept of "civil society" which was currently released in the *Civil Society Index* of the *Open Society Institute* in Sofia, since it encompasses the whole spectrum of the sector (OSI 2011:23). It states that there is still no consistent and generally accepted meaning of "civil society" in Bulgaria and that a *clear-cut* definition of the sector is still lacking (OSI 2011:23). The *Open Society Institute* therefore uses the following definition in its report: "*Civil society is the dynamic arena, outside of the family, the state, and the market, which is created by individual and collective actions, organizations and institutions to advance publicly shared interests"* (OSI 2011:23).

Field data and key informants

My field data were gathered during in September / October 2010 through the use of different ethnographic research methods and added secondary data. I conducted in-depth interviews and structured discussions with four persons, as well as many unstructured interviews and informal talks with my key informants as well as other people that were important for my work.

Choosing partners for my interviews, I tried to find a mix of persons representing internationally established environmentalist organizations like *WWF Bulgaria*, local Bulgarian organizations like *Za Zemiata*[1], civil groups like *Citizens for Rila*[2] and the former grass-roots organization and now political party *Zelenite*[3], in order to gain an overview of the scene. The relatively small number of key informants was to a certain extent counterbalanced by the fact that they were active in more than one institution and could give me a good general overview of institutions, organizations and participants of the "Green scene" in Sofia.

Already existing personal contacts in Sofia enabled me to get in touch with Ivo[4] from *WWF Bulgaria,* who introduced me to many other

1 За Земята, *For the Earth* was registered in 1995 as an environmental non-governmental organization in Bulgaria. It aims mainly at a sustainable life on planet earth. One member of the organization compared them with *Greenpeace* because their areas of interest equally vary between very specific campaigns for the protection of the mountains and more general topics such as climate related issues.

2 The civil group Граждани за Рила, *Citizens for Rila* deals with the protection of the Rila mountains and the Rila National Park from the building of extensive ski resorts. One aim of this civil group is to establish sustainable and alternative tourism in this area.

3 „The Greens" - Зелените

4 All names are fictional to warrant the informants´ anonymity.

people from Green organizations in Sofia. Through the snowball system I met Anton who is a member of the Green political movement called *Zelenite* as well as a member of the Green NGO *Za Zemiata*. Anton is also trying to establish *Green Drinks*[5] in Sofia which is an informal monthly meeting place for people interested in Green issues. Also Rumina is an active member of a group called *Citizens for Rila* and has participated in numerous actions of various other Green organizations in Sofia.

In the field, I used several ethnographic methods, mainly four structured and seven unstructured interviews, one mental map, three free lists and four participant observations, as well as five online questionnaires. I used two types of interviews to find answers to my subsequent questions.

Age distribution	%	Total (N)
20-30	44,4	4
30-40	22,2	2
40-50	11,1	1
50-60	22,2	2
	100	9

Table 1 shows the age range of the interviewed persons. As to be seen in the table, most of the interview partners were between 20-30, meaning they have no direct experience with the socialist past of the country or only experienced the last years of it as young children. This underlines the generational shift in actions and attitudes towards a new era of civic participation.

5 Green Drinks is an informal meeting of people interested in green matters or working in the environmental field, in order to catch up or make new contacts. Green Drinks takes place in cities all over the world. See also www.greendrinks.org

Key informants	Highest educational level	Member of Green organization
Rumina	Masters degree	yes
Anton	Masters degree	yes
Ivo	Masters degree	yes
Nikolai	Masters degree	yes

Table 2 points out that the middle generation engaging in Green civic activism has a high educational level. Their critical attitude may play a sustaining role in determining Bulgaria's future.

It proved to be very helpful to get together with the informants for a first informal meeting before the actual interviews, in order to exchange basic personal information and, to a certain extent, to create a level of trust between the informants and myself. A pre-test of the interviews with personal acquaintances also turned out to be helpful to eliminate ambiguities and potential misunderstandings before the actual interview within the field. However, when transliterating the interviews afterwards I encountered some passages where going into additional details in a second round of interviews would add further to my findings. I also changed the order of some questions after the first interview and added new questions I did not think of at home but got inspiration when in the field.

I made use of participant observation to identify central actors in the field of Green activism. Among other things, I participated in one of the *Green Drinks Sofia* meetings in *The Tea House* at Georgi Benkovski Street, where I was able to get in touch with more people from Sofia's Green scene. Furthermore I attended a staff meeting at the *Future Friendly* Office. The main difficulty here was the language barrier. Most participants knew English quite well but did not feel comfortable enough to hold the whole meeting in a foreign language. Amongst themselves they preferred to communicate in Bulgarian with some translation offered to me. An unexpected experience was the staff meeting of the *Future Friendly* organization, since they held the entire meeting in English to fully include me.

I used free lists in order to find out which Green organizations are to be found in Sofia and mental maps to find out whether there was a visible clustering of "Green places" in Sofia, but my results show there was no such spatial agglomeration. All offices of Green organizations are spread over the entire city center, not located in a specific quarter.

After my return to Hamburg some additional questions occurred, which I presented to my key informants by e-mail. This turned out to be quite efficient and productive, since I got very detailed responses.

A new (and, to me surprising) approach to contact informants was the extensive use of the electronic network *Facebook*. Before the field-work in Bulgaria I had not been a member of this network, but I was told by our Bulgarian fellow students that *Facebook* plays a significant role within the young generation there. As a matter of fact, my partners always asked for my *Facebook* or *Skype* coordinates to exchange information and to stay in contact. Potential new informants and friends of friends were suggested to me on *Facebook*, so I could easily get in contact with them.

Civil society in Bulgaria: the current discourse

As mentioned above, there are still only a few ethnographic case studies of civic movements in Bulgaria, especially of civic activism in the field of environmental protection.

Different overviews and general evaluations of the current situation have been published by Bulgarian offices of international foundations, such as the Friedrich Ebert Stiftung.[6] The Sofia based Center for the

---

6 *Georgiev, Plamen K.* 2009: Bulgarian Political Culture in Change. Sofia: Friedrich Ebert Foundation Office Bulgaria Analyses.

Studies of Democracy (CSD) recently published a brochure on Civil Society in Bulgaria. Trends and Risks[7], which gives detailed insights into the topic but focuses on institutional and legal aspects. The Open Society Institute Sofia published The Civil society Index 2008-2010 in 2011[8]. Sonja Schüler´s (2009) case study about the development of civil society in Bulgaria was particularly helpful, because she uses the example of environmentalism[9].

The current theoretical debate about Bulgaria´s civil society is marked by conflicting theoretical positions.

In the Bulgarian context Francis Fukuyama´s thoughts about "low trust" and "high trust" societies (Fukuyama 1995) are frequently cited, although they do not explicitly refer to Bulgaria. In his book *Trust: The social virtues and the creation of prosperity*, Fukuyama sets out a theory of economic development based on the amount of trust each society has in its institutions (Brewster 1998). He distinguishes between family-centred societies as low trust societies, and institution-centred societies as high trust societies (Fukuyama 1995). His theory of trust supposes cultural habits affecting the amount of family exclusiveness (Brewster 1998). Consequently, the amount of non-kin interaction allows trust in voluntary institutions. Societies with a high level of kin-interactions, according to Fukuyama, tend to have a low level of trust in the state and voluntary associations, whereas states with a low level of kin-interaction tend to have a higher degree of trust.

Furthermore, Fukuyama sees the level of trust as a decisive factor for economic stability and political success of a country, predicting that high

---

Genov, Nikolai 2010: Ups and Downs of Social Democracy in Bulgaria. Sofia: Friedrich Ebert Foundation Office Bulgaria Analyses.

7 *Center for the Study of Democracy* 2010: Civil Society in Bulgaria. Trends and Risks. Sofia.

8 Open Society Institute Sofia 2011: Civil Society Index 2008-2010. Civil Society in Bulgaria: Citizens Actions Without Engagement. Sofia.

9 *Schüler, Sonja* 2009: Zivilgesellschafliche Entwicklungen in Bulgarien am Beispiel Umweltschutz. In: Sterbling, Anton (Ed.), Zivilgesellschafliche Entwicklungen in Südosteuropa. Südosteuropa-Gesellschaft. Munich et al.: Sagner.

trust societies are economically and politically more successful than low trust societies. According to Fukuyama, low trust societies are characterized by small family-based companies, very strong state corruption and small, inefficient organizations (Fukuyama 1995). Within these societies, trust is located almost exclusively in personal relationships (relatives, friends, intimate social networks), while there is a high degree of distrust in the state and its institutions which are perceived as hostile. Social capital is mainly accumulated through the establishment and maintenance of functioning social networks which attain a family-like structure and provide mutual support in case of need. On the contrary, the high trust societies are characterized by large companies with the involvement of non-family members, and an extensive civil society with efficient organizations and lower administration costs. Trust is largely located in abstract institutions, social relations and in the state. The state and the government are generally perceived as legitimate (Fukuyama 1995).

As Christian Giordano (2007) notes however, the terms "low trust" and "high trust society" cannot remain unchallenged. He criticizes Fukuyama's concepts as a deficit-theory (Giordano 2007:21), which clearly is rhetorically effective and in parts scientifically sound, but which also contains an ethnocentric conception focusing too strongly on Western liberal-capitalist models (Giordano 2007:21). I will come back to this criticism in my concluding discussion of Fukuyama´s model applied to a transition society[10] like present-day Bulgaria.

Klaus Roth (Roth 2007, 2009) is carefully optimistic, predicting that institutional trust will slowly increase and that the younger generation has already developed a higher degree of „anonymous trust" (Roth 2007:13). Roth also points to the influence and role of foreign investors as employers in Bulgaria. Bulgarian employees regard them as more

10 The term "transition society" is used to describe the period of transformation from communist rule to democratic and market economy structures in the wake of the political changes in 1989 in Europe.

trustworthy in their corporate social responsibility, thus setting a trend towards a higher degree of institutional trust (Roth 2007:13).

Historical background

The factors determining civil society in Bulgaria today have appreciably been shaped by its specific cultural and historical past. The negative and pessimistic attitude towards the chances of civil society represented in much of the literature, reflects a generalized view of Bulgaria as a country with particularly difficult conditions, characterized by top-down political communication as an aftermath of authoritarian regimes, socialist command systems and deficiencies in the rule of law.

In Bulgarian history, externally imposed command systems like the Ottoman rule and the communist regime engraved a perception of the state as untrustworthy and even inimical to its population (Roth 2007:7). The time between the liberation from the Ottoman rule and the socialist take-over had been too short to generate institutional trust within the population (Roth 2007:10). In the transition phase following the political changes of 1989, criminal structures closely intertwined with state institutions, further enhanced the loss of confidence towards the state and politics in general. Fraud, nepotism and political corruption reached endemic dimensions. In consequence, citizens preferred to exclusively engage for their own interests, resulting in a dramatic trend of withdrawal from public and political life and a shift towards private networks of family, friends and colleagues (Benovska-Sabkova 2007, 2008), (Giordano 2007:26, Roth 2007:7). The widespread distrust regarding the state and its institutions resulted in a marked dichotomy between the private and the public sphere.

Moreover, due to deficient state institutions and economic insecurity, private social networks had been essential for everyday survival before and after the transformation processes after 1989, which consequentially intensified the preservation of these informal networks. Despite this remaining antagonism between the private and the public sphere however, the transformation period after 1989 saw a growing number of NGO registrations, which reflect fundamental changes such as free speech and access to global media.

Roots of the environmental movement

Since my fieldwork specifically focused on the role and perspectives of the environmental movement for civil society in Bulgaria today, it seems necessary to also reflect – as part of the historic background – the historic evolution of the current environmental movement in Bulgaria.

Most authors state that the roots of the Green movement and of environmental organizations in Bulgaria lie within the opposition movement of 1988 in the Ruse area. Protection of the environment and human rights were the first topics of the evolving opposition and substantially contributed to the fall of the communist regime in 1989. In contrast, Barbara Cellarius (2004) dates the origin of environmental activism back much further, stating that "*the environmental movement in Bulgaria sprang to life as a herald of revolutionary social transformation*" (Cellarius 2004:29). She further points out, that although the protest in the Ruse area became the symbol of anti-communist dissent and therefore will always play an important role in the history of the environmental movement in Bulgaria, the history of organizations with environmental purposes go back more than a century (Cellarius 2004:30).

The first legislative measures to protect natural resources appeared the decade following independence in 1878 with the passage of laws on fishing, hunting and forestry. The very first organization with an environmental focus was the *Bulgarian Nature Research Society*, established in 1896. Others such as the *Botanical Society*, *Geographical Society* and the *Union of Foresters* quickly followed. In 1928 the *Union for the Protection of Nature* evolved from nature protection societies and organizations. It played a significant role in creating Bulgaria's first protected areas, as well as the first law on nature conservation within the country (Cellarius 2004:30). In 1934 the Union suggested the creation of the very first national park in Bulgaria on Vitosha Mountain. Another big success was the passing of the law for the protection of Bulgarian nature in 1936, which specified different types of protected territories, for instance reserves, national parks, natural landmarks and natural historical places. However, the actual protection was weak and only little research had been done on the flora and fauna within protected areas.

Nature conservation developments under socialist rule

In the mid-1940s most of the independent nature observation organizations in Bulgaria disappeared or lost their autonomy by being incorporated into or associated with state-controlled organizations (Cellarius 2004:31). The formation of independent NGOs was discouraged and information about environmental issues was frequently suppressed, so citizens were hardly able to influence decision making on environmental matters. Nature conservation received new attention in the 1960s with the passage of a new law on nature protection and the creation of additional protected areas. In 1976 students from the biological faculty at Sofia University established the *Youth Club for the Conservation of Nature* which Cellarius sees as an "ecoglasnost - prototype organization" (Cellarius 2004:34). Despite the decrease of environmental organizations, Bulgaria started to participate in international programs and activities for biodiversity conservation during the socialist era. Various international forums were hosted by Bulgaria between 1984 and 1989 (Cellarius 2004:32).

Ecoglasnost – environmental movements as opposition to communist power

However, people living in the industrial area of Ruse enormously suffered from the air pollution emitted by the big industrial plants. In 1988 the citizens of Ruse started to protest against obsolete industrial enterprises and the lack of a sustainable ecological policy under the communist regime of Todor Zivkov and formed the *Civil Committee for the Ecological Defense of Ruse*. The core members of the *Committee for*

Ruse proceeded to establish the *Independent Union Ecoglasnost (Екогласност)* in 1989 (Cellarius 2004:30, Andonova 2004:154). The Union primarily addressed ecological objectives, but also stated the need for democratic and economic reforms as an important factor for a cleaner environment in Bulgaria. Liliana Andonova states that "*although the frames used in public discourse were pure ecological ones, the unvoiced but obvious long-term aim of most participants [in Ecoglasnost], was, right from the beginning, to be a real opposition to the communist power*" (Andonova 2004:155).

After the fall of the Berlin Wall in 1989, Green movements and parties increased their political influence in Bulgaria. The relatively strong presence of environmental groups in the first post-communist parliament reflected both public concern about the environment and the popularity of *Ecoglasnost* political figures (Andonova 2004:156). Many new local and national organizations with an environmental focus appeared after 1990. Their focus was laid most often on issues that generated international funding, such as the conservation of biological diversity, public education on environmental matters, anti-nuclear activities, as well as local environmental problems (Andonova 2004:156).

However, the upcoming "*fragmentation, political manoeuvring, and ideological squabbles*" (Andonova 2004:156) among the environmental organizations vastly weakened the Green movement at that time. Moreover, in consequence of the increasing socioeconomic crisis the environmental objectives were overshadowed by difficult economic reforms. The enthusiasm of the early transition period and the interest for environmental matters of the Bulgarian population diminished and numerous organizations gave up their involvement. Andonova points out that there were "*positive changes in the making of environmental policy*" but a strong institutional capacity and legislative changes could not be established.

The environmental movement enjoyed a revival at the end of the 1990s. New challenges for the Bulgarian nature and environmental requirements for EU accession brought the topic back into focus. Moreover, new communication tools such as mobile phones and the internet made it much easier to network. Various new organizations and civil groups arose, and particularly the young generation participated. In some cases they even formed coalitions. A unitary Green party however never emerged in Bulgaria. Some efforts were to be seen, even a selective involvement with the European Greens, but this was never reflected in serious actions or an active participation within the Bulgarian National Assembly.

Recent developments: grass-roots movement vs. PONGOs

Lately, a new and promising development can be observed with the emergence of grassroots structures such as a new Green party called *Zelenite*. However, the problem of nepotism has remained an issue until today. Many Bulgarians do not trust NGOs without reserves, which makes private funding rather difficult. This is mainly due to clientelism and corruption within the third sector (CSD 2010:28) and the appearance of the so-called PONGOs (Political NGOs). Because of the enticement of funding, municipal officials take advantage of the inadequate regulatory framework of the third sector which allows them to become members of the managing boards of non-profit organizations, as there are no regulations or auditing concerning the participations of municipalities in civic organizations (CSD 2010:27). An indirect evidence of NGO capture is the boom in registrations. The number of NGOs registrations increased eight-fold between 2000 and 2010 (CSD 2010:27). According to the Center of the Studies for Democracy, 79% of the members of the 2005-2009 parliament and 90% of municipality mayors were members of managing boards of NGOs at the end of 2008. Apparently some mayors gave up their position in a non-profit organization but installed close friends instead (CSD 2010:28) "PONGOs are *undermining the very nature of non-profits by risking to turn them into a cover up for a white collar crime*" (CSD 2010:27).

Discussion of field data

The data gathered during my field work seem to support the general impression drawn from the literature. Although there are signs of an increasing involvement with environmentalist issues, the evolving activism is still characterized by significant problems.

Recruiting members

A major topic in my field data is the fundamental difficulty of Green organizations in recruiting a sufficient number of new members. I was told by all of my informants that the support for Green NGOs is generally and gradually increasing, but it was also obvious that most groups had problems with a structured acquisition of members.

Ivo from *WWF* - traditionally strong in members all over the world - told me in an unrecorded talk, that even his organization has trouble with establishing a functioning and efficient membership structure. Membership is a decisive factor for all such organizations not only because of the necessary cash flow for logistics and promotional activities (assemblies, office infrastructure, promoting public activities and actions etc.), but also in terms of credibility and capacity.

What is missing is a structured procedure to recruit members. Apparently it is still difficult to motivate potential members, not only the environmentalists´ own peer group. According to a statement of one of my key informants, many young people just do not like the negative tone of a protest movement and lack the necessary patience for sustainable approaches. They rather want to see instant results of any action. Protests are always linked with the expectation that politicians can be influenced and convinced to change their previous course of action. The difficulty is, that most of the Bulgarians still do not have much faith in politicians and political parties.

Moreover, the members of the active core of the organizations I studied told me that most Bulgarians are still not used to civil movements, have not been educated in democratic processes and need inspiration to act. They do not see themselves as equal, fully integrated members of society and somehow feel unqualified to actively influence others. In contrast they see the members of organizations as experts and some sort of leaders whom they may occasionally support, but do not see a way to personally engage in an inclusive manner. These are still signs of the lack of a democratic tradition and an insufficient education in this regard.

Information and mutual exchange

However, my participants also admitted that there is a lack of communication and public information on the part of their organizations. People who are not closely involved with the environmental scene or who do not have special access to information through specific institutions often cannot get detailed information. Another impediment is that the existing local organizations do not sufficiently work together and do not form networks. According to all of my informants, this is generally to be seen as a problem of civil society in Bulgaria. *"Although the motto on the facade of the National Assembly says 'Unity makes strength', the Bulgarians are exceptional as individuals but taken together they are no good at all"* (Daily News, Dec. 2010:7), said Dr. Konstantin Trenchev, leader of the *Podkrepa Labour Confederation*[11] in an interview for the English speaking newspaper of the Bulgarian News Agency in December 2010. Trenchev is convinced that it will take a long time to outlive this "*individualistic syndrome*" (Daily News, Dec. 2010:7).

Whether sufficient common grounds for a better networking can be established in Bulgaria is still to be seen, and most likely it is a question of gradual generational change. However, I noticed the same propensity Trenchev pictures during my stay in Bulgaria in 2010. When I asked Ivo about the overall goals of the environmental organization in which he is working full time, he was only able to name the goals of his own

11 Podkrepa Labour Confideration is a bulgarian trade union. It was founded in 1989 and is affiliated with the International Trade Union Confederation and the European Trade Union Confederation.

workspace but not the ones of his colleagues he shares an office with. He was quite astonished by this himself and immediately asked his colleagues if they knew what he was currently working on, but indeed they did not.

Cooperation and networking

As I mentioned before, it became apparent that the local NGOs do not regularly cooperate. Collaborative and joint actions or protests are still an exception rather than the rule. One impediment seems to be the strong self-will, Dr. Trenchev refers to (Daily News, dec 2010:7). Individual organizations tend to believe that their task or field of activism is far more important than the focus of other organizations, even though all topics are environmentally oriented. I often heard from my informants that this problem is mostly due to a lack of long-term strategies worked out within the organizations.

Resources and reputation

This phenomenon is aggravated by the continuous fight for resources between organizations. As mentioned above, many Bulgarians do not trust NGOs without reservation, due to the undermining character of the PONGOs, which makes private funding rather difficult. These tendencies outline a serious peril to the development of independent NGOs, as well as to the reputation of civil society in Bulgaria.

When talking about reputation, my participants made clear that there is an inevitable connection between an organization´s expertise and its public perception as being trustworthy. In order to overcome the widespread reservations against political institutions, they must present extensive knowledge about the issues they criticize and campaign on. One the one hand, this expertise ensures effective campaigns and educational programs. On the other hand, it increases the problems of recruiting new members by perpetuating the hierarchy between "expert" activists and "lay" public.

Civic activism and institutionalized politics

The problem of insufficient collaboration within the environmentalist movement is also reflected in the interplay between the political sphere and non-governmental activism. As the CSD report on civil society in Bulgaria today states, some "*patronizing streaks*" are still observable as a leftover from communist times in the attitudes of the political establishment towards NGOs (CSD 2010:25). Most environmental organizations in Sofia maintain relationships with the *Ministry of Environment and Water*[12]. However, as in most of their actions, these connections are not based on a long term strategy, but remain rather sporadic.

It appears that usually the organizations initiate these collaborations, whereas the government rather tries to keep them out of the business. However, despite these tendencies it became apparent during my research that, although slowly, an interest in institutionalized politics seems to be increasing again among activists.

A generational shift is visible in the public perception of politics in the case of the young political party *Zelenite*, in which young people from Sofia begin to take responsibility and engage in the sphere of party politics. This could possibly be a sign that exclusive instruments of political power and non-transparent decision making are no longer, or at least decreasingly, tolerated in the post-accession EU context (Georgiev 2009:10). This could to some extent further stimulate civil society and set the tone for younger or future generations, but it is too early to assess the sustainability of such trends.

Stories of success: managing new forms of communication

An increasingly important factor for the work of environmentalist organizations in Bulgaria today are new communication technologies which have only been introduced in the past few years. The organizations

12 Министерството на околната среда и водите

have made good use of them, thus creating a new platform for civic initiatives. An outstanding and often cited example is the *BG Mamma* platform[13]. In 2002 *BG Mamma* became the first Bulgarian internet portal entirely dedicated to childcare. A few months later a forum was started as a part of the website which quickly gained popularity. As of June 2010, *BG Mamma* is the largest portal related to maternity. There are 113.000 registered users and about 2.000.000 discussion topics. Furthermore, it is not only a virtual phenomenon. The users take an active stand on current affairs and organize protest actions also on environmental issues (CSD 2010:60).

The *Natura 2000* protest actions were mentioned in all of my interviews. The following example highlights one of the little victories of the environmental scene in the past and thus demonstrates the pressure civic groups are able to exert on the political scenery, if they appear as a unified group and act strategically.

Natura 2000 is an ecological network of protected areas in the territory of the EU. In 2007, scientists mandated by the EU proposed that around 60% of the Bulgarian territory should become a protected area and therefore part of the *Natura 2000* network. The government back then refused to accept the 60% and cut the percentage back to 12 %. This provoked massive protests of environmentalists including all of my key informants. One of them even played an outstanding role in this context, since he actively tried to bring politicians and environmentalist together to talk about the *Natura 2000* issue.

13 www.bg-mamma.com

High media attention in front of the Council of Ministers (photo: M. C. Höpfner).

Together with activists from the biological faculty of Sofia University, he started a permanent protest against these cuts in front of the Council of Ministers, which should last nine months. Many more Green organizations joined in the protest. In the end, 32% of the areas proposed by the network were accepted by the government. The environmentalists are still fighting for a few zones. Obviously the help of the European Commission played a role here too, but the mobilization of Bulgarian citizens and the stamina the activists showed displayed how seriously they took this environmental problem.

In March 2011, a few months after my fieldwork, an informant told me about major demonstrations of anti-nuclear activists in front of the Council of Ministers protesting against the project of a new nuclear power plant in Belene. This time, *Zelenite* managed to include a number of other organizations and an overall number of approximately 1000 protesters was reported, an impressive number for Bulgaria. This could potentially be the beginning of a wind of change in favor of the environmental movement, since the opinion polls have changed from 80/20 % pro Belene to 50/50% in the aftermath of the Fukushima disaster in Japan.

Conclusions: applications and limits of Fukuyama's model of "trust"

In my fieldwork, I focused on environmentalism as a specific area of civic participation in Bulgaria, looking for indications for an increasing involvement with civil society. Based on my field data, several indicators seem to corroborate this.

I agree with Klaus Roth, who stated that the younger generation (20-40) already possesses a higher degree of *anonymous trust* (Roth 2007:13). But could personal networking and personal friendship possibly also be seen as an asset in the context of an emerging civil society in Bulgaria, rather than being qualified as typical low-trust characteristics?

As Klaus Roth stated in 2007, the "*entire social life has a binary structure, consisting of two clearly separated spaces to which people attach very different values*" and "*the private space is the life world for which the individual really cares and feels responsibility and attachment [...] he or she invests most of his or her time and resources*" for the private space (Roth 2007: 8). Moreover the public sphere, according to Roth, begins "*right outside one's own doorsteps; spatially it includes already the staircase and the space around the apartment blocks or the house just as well as the streets and places [...]*" (Roth 2007: 8).

However, networks consisting of family and close friends are not the only important ones. Trust is also imposed on other relations. According to Benovska-Sabkova (2007:153), friendship has been a common principle and form of social organization during socialist and post-socialist time. "*You know if someone is your true friend when you are in need*" is a popular Bulgarian proverb (Benovska-Sabkova 2007: 147).

People could rely on their social networks, no matter how often they actually see each other.

My own observations among environmentalist activists in Sofia 2010 do not fully support Roth´s assumption of a *sharp opposition* (Roth 2007:7) between the private and the public sphere, at least within the younger generation (20-40). Many activist organizations are formed of friends, schoolmates, colleagues or fellow students. Consequently the people within the organizations know each other well and have a common ground of trust preceding the actual cause they are rallying for. I therefore agree with Christian Giordano at this point, who states that the traditionally strong role of the family in southeastern Europe societies must be taken into account, without overemphasizing family and kin relationships (Giordano 2004:329, 2010).

It is true that many of the organizations I got to know had their roots in pre-existing social networks of fellow students or old school friends, but making use of personal networks in the context of Bulgaria's civil society today is not necessarily a sign of *low trust*. First and foremost, Bulgaria's young generation is mixing available networks in order to gain the most efficient outcome in their work within the Green scene.

In conclusion, I argue that although Fukuyama's theory may be principally applicable to the case of Bulgaria, its application must be more differentiated in the recent Bulgarian context. As the example of *Zelenite*, as well as examples of civic groups engaging in neighborhood issues clearly show, in the younger generation the spheres of *private* and *public* are not as definitely separated anymore as used to be expected. In analyzing the chances of civil society involvement in Bulgaria, the younger generation has to be clearly taken into account.

Personal ties and informal networks should not only be seen as typical *low trust* elements, but may in fact form a catalyst for the unfolding of civil society, if favorable circumstances prevail. In the case of Bulgaria, such favorable circumstances may arise due to the country's new European status that enhances a willingness to catch up with civil society rights and responsibilities (Georgiev 2009: 10).

The Green movement has clearly shifted from being a "*mobilization agent for populist protests*" (Jancar-Webster 1998: 69) in the end of the communist era to a more pragmatic, goal-oriented one. Georgiev states in his analysis that the civic culture in Bulgaria has reached a decisive turning point, since it is now related to the notion of "what should happen" and, in that sense, moving towards long desired social and democratic changes (Georgiev 2009: 10). The further involvement of young and middle-aged generations with a high educational level and a critical attitude will certainly play a sustaining role in determining Bulgaria's future. Civic culture of an activist participatory type seems a major force to foster significant changes (Georgiev 2009: 12).

However, it seems necessary to also highlight the interdependency between civil society capacity on the one hand and the rule of law on the other. A constructive civil society evolvement can be heavily impaired by serious deficiencies of the law enforcement system. The fact that such serious deficiencies continue to exist in Bulgaria, monitored by the European Unions' Cooperation and Verification Mechanism (CVM)[14] indicates that the new trends of Bulgarian civil society as outlined above are still on shaky grounds. Still endemic corruption and continuing organized crime criticized by the EU in the biannual CVM progress reports, as well as monopolistic tendencies resulting from oligarch-style economic conglomerates of the earlier transition period and their networking with the political and judicial system, continue to frustrate hopes for state accountability and justice[15].

One of the challenges will be the restoration of institutional trust and the rule of law. At the same time, improvements of the rule of law in

14 Report from the Commission to the European Parliament and the Council on Progress in Bulgaria under the Co-operation and Verification Mechanism. Brussels. 20.07.2011

15 Center for the Study of Democracy 2009: Crime without Punishment, Countering Corruption and Organized Crime in Bulgaria. Sofia.
Center for the Study of Democracy 2010: Examining the Links Between Organized Crime and Corruption. Sofia.

Bulgaria will only be sustainable if civil society adopts a more active role of civic monitoring. Much will therefore depend on the success of the European Union to help Bulgaria meet the requirements of the CVM. Nevertheless, a positive start of a new civil society dynamism in Bulgaria can be observed that in combination with a generational change gives reason to careful optimism.

Continued scrutiny through empirical fieldwork and scientific analysis of civil society trends in Bulgaria also beyond the environmental movement seems well worthwhile.

References

Andonova, Liliana (2004) Bulgaria: Harmonization without Implementation. In: Andonova, Liliana (ed.) Transnational Politics of the Environment. The EU and Environmental Policy in Central Eastern Europe. Cambridge: MIT Press.

Benovskava-Sabkova, Milena (2007) Friendship and Friendly Coalitions and Groups. Friendship as a Pattern of Social Relations. In: Roth, Klaus (Ed.), Soziale Netzwerke und Soziales Vertrauen in den Transformationsländern. Vienna et al.: 143-153.

— (2008) Leisure Time, Friendship Groups and Social Capital in Bulgaria. Examples from the Socialist and the Post-Socialist Period. In: Roth, Klaus (ed.), Sozialkapital-Vertrauen-Rechtssicherheit. Vienna et al.: 183-204.

Brewster, Dennis R. (1998) A Theory of Trust. An Exposition of Francis Fukuyama's "Trust". Corpus Christi, Texas. Electronic document: http://webpages.charter.net/dbrews/trust.htm [15.11.2011, 11:57].

Cellarius, Barbara A. (2004) In the Land of Orpheus. Rural Livelihood and Nature Conservation in Postsocialist Bulgaria. Madison: University of Wisconsin Press.

Center for the Study of Democracy.(2009) Crime without Punishment, Countering Corruption and Organized Crime in Bulgaria. Sofia.

— (2010) Civil Society in Bulgaria. Trends and Risks. Sofia.

— (2010) Examining the Links Between Organized Crime and Corruption. Sofia.

Daily News, No. 291, 15. December 2010. Sofia: 7-8.

Fukuyama, Francis (1995) Social Capital and the global economy. In: Foreign Affairs.

Georgiev, Plamen K. (2009) Bulgarian Political Culture in Change. Sofia: Friedrich Ebert Foundation Office Bulgaria Analyses.

Genov, Nikolai (2010) Ups and Downs of Social Democracy in Bulgaria. Sofia: Friedrich Ebert Foundation Office Bulgaria Analyses.

Giordano, Christian (2004): Das entfremdete Gemeinwohl: Zur sozialen Produktion von Misstrauen in Gesellschaften am Rande Europas. In: Bonvin, Jean-Michel, Georg Kohler and Beat Sitter-Liver (eds.): Gemeinwohl — bien commun. Ein kritisches Plädoyer — Un plaidoyer critique. Fribourg: 325 – 351.

— (2007) Privates Vertrauen und informelle Netzwerke: Zur Organisationskultur in Gesellschaften des öffentlichen Misstrauens. Südosteurops im Blickpunkt. In: Roth, Klaus (ed.), Soziale Netzwerke und Soziales Vertrauen in den Transformationsländern. Vienna et al.: 22-47.

— (2010) Why New Agrarian Capitalist are Successful in Bulgaria: The Relevance of Personalized Social Networks and Face to Face Trust Relations. Ethnoscripts, 12, 2010: 15-33.

Jancar-Webster, Barbara (1998) Environmental Movements and Social Change in the Transisition Countries. In: Baker, Susan (ed.) 1998: Dilemmas of Transition. The Environment, Democracy and Economic Reform in Eastern Europe. London: 69-89.

Roth, Klaus (2007) Trust, Networks and Social Capital in the Transformation Countries. In: Roth, Klaus (ed.), Soziale Netzwerke und Soziales Vertrauen in den Transformationsländern. Vienna et al.: 6-19.

— (2009) Zivilgesellschaft in Südosteuropa? Beobachtungen aus ethnologischer Sicht. In: Sterbling, Anton (ed.), Zivilgesellschafliche Entwicklungen in Südosteuropa. Südosteuropa-Gesellschaft. Munich et al.

Open Society Institute Sofia (2011) Civil Society Index 2008-2010. Civil Society in Bulgaria: Citizen Actions Without Engagement. Sofia.

Schüler, Sonja (2009) Zivilgesellschafliche Entwicklungen in Bulgarien am Beispiel Umweltschutz. In: Sterbling, Anton (Ed.), Zivilgesellschafliche Entwicklungen in Südosteuropa. Südosteuropa-Gesellschaft. Munich et al.

— (2009) Civil Society in Bulgaria after 1989 - Characteristics and Developments. In: Voß, Christian (ed.): EU – Bulgaristik. Perspektiven und Potentiale. Munich et al.

The daily work in small cafés in Sofia

Renate Kleinknecht

After the fall of the socialist regime in 1989, Bulgaria pursued a strategy of promoting small firms, i.e. companies with up to 20 employees and an annual turnover of up to 1.000 000 Bulgarian Leva[1], aiming to support the labour market, to raise export quota and to encourage investments. Since 1989 small firms have been dominating the economy in Bulgaria, most of them in trade and service (Dittrich et al. 2006: 29ff.). My research deals with small cafés as a particular form of small entrepreneurship.

In the centre of Sofia many small cafés, bistros and bars are located. According to Christian Gehl (2008: 71), on entering Bulgaria two things attract particular attention – the elegantly dressed women and the fully occupied cafés. It seems to be a favourite pastime in Sofia to sit together around a café table, to talk and to drink coffee.

This inspired me to investigate cafés as a special form of small entrepreneurship on the one hand, and as a cultural domain on the other. It is relatively easy to establish this type of business, because there is no need for high investments (e.g. in special kitchen equipment) and it is possible to run a small café without additional staff. In my fieldwork, my main interest focused on the practice and organization of everyday work. During my research I observed the work routines in two cafés in Sofia and I conducted interviews with owners, employees and customers.

From coffee house to café: historical background

European coffee house culture dates back to the 16th century, rooted in the Arabic habit to drink "Qahva", a drink from the roast seeds of the coffee plant. Especially religious groups favoured the "Qahva" because the intoxicating effect of caffeine led to the assumption to be closer to

1 1 Lev (BGN) = 0.511 € (www.bankenverband.de, 5. Oktober 2011).

divine beings. A spiritual power was attributed to this drink which encouraged concentration and active discussions. In Istanbul, the first public coffee house was established in 1554 and soon, coffee houses became socially accepted institutions (Thiele-Dohrmann 1997: 7 ff).

"Café Viva": the guest room (photo: R. Kleinknecht)

During the Ottoman era, coffee arrived in Europe. In 1626, the first coffee house was established in Venice. From there, the habit spread across Europe via Vienna and Budapest. In 1900, Budapest alone had 600 cafés (Thiele-Dohrmann 1997: S. 7 ff). Especially in Vienna, coffee houses developed a variety of preparations similar to the various coffee drinks in Italy, but cafés offered much more than just different kinds of coffee. They served – and still serve – as informal meeting places. During the 19th and 20th century, certain cafés became a focus for particular lifestyles. Cafés were created as confectioneries, as meeting places for poets with sheets of paper and pencils for the writing guests, as artists´ cafés, for businessmen with newspapers provided, or as meeting points for political discussions. Not surprisingly, some guests may stay in a café house for hours, just drinking one single cup of coffee (Thiele-Dohrmann 1997).

Small firms and labour in Bulgaria

Until 1989, economic policy in Bulgaria was based on state directives and characterized by a high dependence on the former USSR. A major factor of the Bulgarian economy was agricultural production in state estates, particularly of export products like tobacco, wheat and vegetables. Industrial production was limited to energy-intensive sectors of heavy industry, which was no longer competitive on an international market after 1990. Private entrepreneurship did not play any significant role.

After 1989, the former export markets for Bulgarian industrial products broke down and a major part of Bulgaria´s industrial infrastructure became obsolete. In the time of transition, the economy was characterized by insufficient technology development, severe environmental problems, high unemployment and a lack of experience with private entrepreneurship, on the side of the owners as well as of the employees (Knaus 1997: 113 ff.).

The political answer to these economic problems was a decree to support small firms. Already in January 1989, the government under Zivkov had passed a law to legitimize the establishment of small firms with up to 20 permanent employees and an expected turn over not higher than 1.000 000 Bulgarian Leva. In February 1990, 11.285 new private enterprises had been founded, most of them owner only. New laws were passed to build a framework for these newly-created enterprises, allowing private ownership of property and farmland, foreign investments and privatisation. An important step was a resolution which provided the return of expropriated property and, along with other changes, formed a basis for the establishment of small firms (Bartlett, Rangelova 1997: 319-333).

According to the National Statistical Institute, 97 % of the Bulgarian companies in the sector of gastronomy in the year 1999 were micro enterprises (Dittrich et al.2006: 29 ff). The situation of these small firms was characterised by a lack of experience with private entrepreneurship at a time of mass privatisation. Some new owners (mainly those with an academic education) tended to invest into the development of their enterprises in order to maximise profits, although high taxes and bureaucratic obstacles complicated success-oriented management strategies.

For the majority of entrepreneurs however, the historic and cultural imprint of the socialist era had a different outcome regarding business management. In those small firms, the relations between employees and employers remained on a familial level. Rates of income did not differ substantially between owners and employees. Even in difficult conditions, employees would not leave their enterprise for reasons of loyalty. Hierarchical structures were virtually non-existent. This concept of enterprise was characterized by a mixture of professional and private life. Another important factor in this form of business is the permanent customer. He is in contact with both the owner and the employee. This concept of enterprise has been described as a significant cultural component in Bulgaria as opposed to other countries (Bartlett, Rangelova 1997: 319–333).

Labour relations in Bulgaria after 1990 have been marked by conditions of work during socialism, when working relationships were long-lasting and – at least officially – there was no unemployment. The socialist regime encouraged close personal relationships between the employees, e.g. by sponsoring celebrations in state enterprises. In consequence, the borders between private time and labour time became quite fluid (Benovska-Sabkova 2004, 2008). The daily work was performed within personalized social networks with a high level of trust;

these "trust-relationships" compensated at least partially for the low level of trust towards the wider society and state institutions (Bartlett, Rangelova 1997: 319-333).

In general, structures and relationships on the workplace have remained quite similar after the transition. There is still a high level of distrust in official politics and state institutions. In consequence, employees are looking for help among their colleagues in instrumental and personal problems. This mutual aid remains an important aspect of every day work.

Small firms in Bulgaria are generally not connected through specific business networks. If private relations exist among the owners, they are not sufficient to encourage economic co-operation. For a more successful management of Bulgarian small firms, specific networks for local, financial and economic support would have to be created (Bartlett, Rangelova 1997: 319 – 333)

Data from the field

During the era of post-socialist transition in Bulgaria, opening a café looked seemed to offer good possibilities to gain an income with relatively low investments. No particular training was necessary to open a coffee house. A small café can be established even in limited space, as it does not need special equipment such as a restaurant kitchen, and it can be run with few staff or by the owners alone.

In my fieldwork, I investigated two small cafés that had been founded under such conditions. My main questions referred to the processes of daily work and to relations between owners, employees and customers. As Benovska-Sabkova (2004, 2008), Petrova (2010) and others have pointed out, the culture of work in Bulgaria has been characterized by an overlapping of the spheres of work and of "private life" or leisure, during as well as after socialist times. In my research, I also set a particular focus on the relations of work and leisure among owners and employees.

During the time of my fieldwork, I conducted regular observations (non-participant, except for my role as a customer) and interviews in two cafés, which are documented in twenty observation protocols. In twelve interviews I asked questions about the enterprises´ history, management, relations between work and free time, suppliers and customers. Every day I visited both cafés and during my stay I observed the daily work and the interactions between employees, owners, customers, suppliers and other persons. I investigated the working day, the duties during the day, the communication and ways to find solutions to problems. I visited both cafés several times a day during the week and on weekends, in order to get an overview of the working days and of the differences between days within the week.

The cafés: places and key informants

Case 1: "Café Rosa"

"Café Rosa", an enterprise with 13 employees, is located in a two-story building in the centre of Sofia, close to the main shopping mile "Boulevard Vitosha". It is not easy to notice the café, because it is somewhat hidden in a side street backyard, with only one sign in that street announcing its location. It is surrounded by a garden with seven tables. Inside the building, the kitchen is located on the ground level, as well as the bar and four tables for guests. On the first floor, there is a smoking area with three rooms with nine tables in total.

"Café Rosa" offers cakes, croissants, several types of coffee and soft drinks. All cakes and croissants are home-made of "biological" ingredients. The employees work in shifts and in different positions. Four bakers prepare the cakes, two waitresses serve the customers and are supported by two managers, who have the task of administrating the receipts. Three barmen prepare the drinks and do the dishes.

"Café Rosa": the garden (photo: R. Kleinknecht)

On sunny days, most of the customers sit outside and some of them come several times a day, drinking just one coffee and staying for hours. The staff is advised to serve, to be friendly and, apart from that, to leave them alone. The customers are mainly permanent clients from the surrounding area, sometimes tourists. At the weekends, the café is frequented by many customers, but in the early morning and in the early evening, there is not much to do and the employees spend time with each other. The café also sells on order and "to go", so some customers just come to take cakes or croissants even though the café has no extra pastry shop.

T. and I. were the two most important informants in "Café Rosa". T. was born in Bulgaria, is 22 years old and lives with her family in Sofia. She has been working as a manager in this café for two years. I. was born in Sofia, is 37 years old and lives as a single in Sofia. He is a barman in the café and has also a job in a wine shop.

Case 2: Café Viva

"Café Viva" is located on the outskirts of the city centre on a silent small street. There is no garden space and just one room with seven tables for guests and a small bar in the cellar with a sales room and a few places at the bar. It is owned by a married couple and had no other employees at the time of my fieldwork. The owners work in two shifts, Sasha (born in Sofia, 48 years old) from 6:30 to 14:00, her husband Lubo (born in Sofia, 52 years old) from 14:00 to 22:00 o'clock. They do all tasks by themselves. The café offers several types of coffee, sandwiches, sweets, soft drinks and alcoholic drinks.

Entrance to „Café Viva" (photo: R. Kleinknecht)

Nearly all clients are permanent customers and visit the café every day, many of them up to two or three times a day. There is a close relationship between the owners and the customers as well as among the customers. Frequently, customers drop by for a talk with the owners and permanent clients support them by serving themselves.

Daily work routines

During my field research, my main interest was to investigate the relationship between work and free time in the context of small enterprises. Ivanka Petrova states: "*Also in the small enterprises of the private sector in the post socialist-period, this intertwining has largely been characteristic of relations among colleagues, between the head and the subordinate, as well as the contacts with partners and customers*" (Petrova 2010: 44). In this article, both cases will be presented as supporting Petrova´s argument. The daily work in both cafés reflects a mixture of professional and private relationships. On the one hand, establishing personal relations may serve as a strategy to oblige the customers to the enterprises. On the other hand, strong personal ties at the workplace are a consequence of long working days, which limit the possibilities to cultivate friendships outside of work.

As Bartlett and Rangelova (1997) have argued, the socialist period was characterized by strong notions of equality at the workplace. As several observations in "Café Rosa" showed me, this notion still exists. Even though there are structural hierarchies among the thirteen employees, they are not reflected in their practical interactions. In "Café Rosa", the daily routine is structured by a working schedule which reflects the different positions and specializations:

Position	Tasks	Working time
owner	control function	not accurately defined
manager	administration	14 hours on 2 days, 2 days free
bartender	preparing the drinks	6 hours a day
waitress	service	14 hours on 2 days, 2 days free
baker	preparing the cakes	6 hours a day

Table 1: positions and work schedule

As Table 1 shows, in principle there is a hierarchical structure of positions, but the daily work shows another picture. No one gives orders to a colleague. Everyone is free to take breaks without asking for permission, and to administer or change their own working hours by writing them into a book that is placed inside the bar. Only the managers however are allowed to disperse the tips and to put the cash and the receipts into a safe. The manager, the barman and the waitress are indoors or in the garden most of the working time, while the baker only works in the kitchen. In the course of a day, customers come and go. They sit down, order drinks and cakes or buy "to go". Every employee, excluding the baker, may take orders and serve the guests. This becomes particularly obvious when a customer wants to buy cake "to go". In these cases at least three employees - manager, barman and waitress - arrange themselves around the customer and everyone takes part in the interaction.

No one gives orders to other colleagues or decides about their working times or breaks. Everyone organises their tasks by him- or herself. The same applies to the administration or to changes of working hours. Inside the bar a book with a working hours plan is disposed and the employees organize the schedules by themselves, e.g. by changing their working times. One hierarchical difference between managers and waitresses appears however, in that the managers are allowed to disperse the tips and to put the cash receipts into a safe. Apart from that, no obvious hierarchy could be observed.

Even though there are no employees in "Café Viva", a division of tasks and a structured working schedule can be recognised. Lubo calls his wife, who is the official owner, "the boss". Also in her own opinion, she is the one who has a better overview and know-how about management and administration.

Inside "Café Viva" (photo: R. Kleinknecht)

Table 2 also shows a clear structure of tasks and working time. The daily work starts at 6:30 a.m., when Sasha arrives to prepare the cafe for the first customers. Many customers drink their first coffee before their work begins. During the morning, customers come and go, taking a coffee or sweets. Most clients visit the café at lunchtime until 2 p.m. Lubo arrives at this hour, and this is also the time for deliveries. Both Sasha and Lubo are present during delivery time and deal with it in equal ways Afterwards Sasha goes home to do chores, administrative work for the café or to support her mother who was sick at the time of my field work. Lubo stays in the café until 10 p.m. serving the customers. In the evening he cleans up and prepares everything for the next day.

Actor	Task	Working time
Sasha	service, administration, receives deliveries	8 hours a day in the café 6:30 a.m. to 2:30 p.m. 2 hours a day administration
Lubo	service, arranges and receives deliveries, cleans the rooms	8 hours a day 2 p.m. to 10 p.m.

Table 2: tasks and work schedule

Relating to customers and colleagues

Relations between owners or staff and the customers vary between both cases. In contrast to "Café Rosa", where the employees are advised to keep their distance to the customers, many customers visit "Café Viva" explicitly to have a conversation with the owner. Before sitting down in the ground floor guest room, regular clients descend into the basement first to greet her, or have longer chats with her. Newly arriving customers may join into these talks, which last between thirty minutes to an hour. According to Sasha, these social interactions are a more important part of her work than, for example, doing administrative duties (Interview with Sasha 27.09.10). Although she is the main contact person, the situation is rather similar during her husband´s working hours from 2 to 10 pm. Also when he is present, customers usually stay in the basement for a while before they go upstairs to sit in the café room.

This practice reflects an intertwining of professional and private contacts which not only arises from working long hours without relief by additional staff, but which can also be seen as a business strategy. Building personal relations effectively binds regular customers to "Café Viva". In my interviews, regular clients stressed that they do not visit competing cafés. The personalized relations between owners and customers are also highlighted by the fact that the owners are very proud that they do not accept tips.

As mentioned before, in "Café Viva" there is no such overlap between private and professional interactions with the customers, but it is clearly visible in the relationships between colleagues. As one of the consequences of the long working hours, employees tend to fill gaps during the day with private activities and private talks among co-workers. During my stays in the café, I was frequently invited by the employees to join these conversations. As they put it, I had become a part of "the team", which meant not just the working team, but rather a private circle.

Other private activities such as shopping or running errands in the city centre, are also done during working hours, because the employees have no fixed breaks. Often they give to each other practical support, such as doing small repairs for each other in the back rooms of the café.

In "Café Viva", instrumental support was also occasionally offered by customers. During one of my visits, a water tap was rusty and defect and the owner waited for her husband to repair it. Eventually he arrvied and tried, but without success, so he asked a regular customer to help. This customer also did not manage and the rusty water tap broke off completely, when another customer came in and also tried in vain to repair it. After a while, the customers advised the owners to ask a neighbour for pliers and new material. While Lubo had gone to the neighbour, four more customers tried their luck, again without success. At last, Lubo managed to repair the tap with the help of the neighbour´s tools and material.

According to theories of the importance of social networks in small firms, I also expected personal contacts or network relations to the suppliers of the cafés. Surprisingly, this was not the case. Both cafés have found their suppliers through their advertisements on the internet. The relationships to the suppliers are not very close. They deliver the goods, talk a few words and go. I did not find closer relationships between the cafés and the suppliers, as well as to other enterprises. In both cases, social networks remain internal, as between the owner and customers in café Viva and among the employees in café Rosa. Although socially very important to the individual actors, these networks are too limited to contribute to the development of new business strategies.

Social relations and economic success

The two cases presented here differ clearly in their economic situation. "Café Viva" offers a comparatively limited range of goods: coffee, cappuccino, espresso, soft drinks, alcoholics, sandwiches and sweets at low prices. Customers pay 70 Stotinki for a cup of coffee, while in "Cafè Rosa" a cup of coffee costs 2 Leva[2]. Many customers stay for hours, drinking just one cup of coffee. According to the owners, their income is hardly sufficient for survival, without a possibility to make enough profit to invest in long-term business improvements.

This café is open almost every day. The owners have no chance to go on holidays, because there are not enough resources to pay for a substitute. Another reason is the dependency on the customers: besides

2 70 Stotinki = 0,35 €, 2 Bulgarian Leva = 1,00 €

the low prices, regular clients visit the café mainly because of the friendly relations with the owners, so during a longer absence they could also lose their regular customers.

In contrast, “Café Rosa” was created by a young couple who had been able to invest money they inherited and who had a vision to develop the enterprise, which is reflected in the daily work schedule. From the beginning, a strong emphasis was laid on aesthetic features such as the garden and a comfortable interior. Also the use of “biological” ingredients is important to the owners. The customers are to feel comfortable and to have a good time. The prices are about 50% higher than in “Café Viva”, but the daily turnover in „Café Rosa“ amounts to about 1.000 Leva, while „Café Viva`s“ daily turnover is only about 500 Leva (Interviews 23.09.10 and 27.09.10).

The café as a cultural domain

Free listing was administered to owners, employees and customers in order to investigate the concept of "café" and the meanings associated with the café as a working place or as a place to relax and to enjoy a variety of offered goods. I collected free lists from eight different informants (two customers, one owner and six employees) with the questions: "*What is a café? Please name everything you associate with this term...*".

Informant	Interior	Goods	Work Place	Meetingpoint
1 (employee)	2	4	1	8
2(employee)	-	-	4	1
3(employee)	-	-	-	9
4(customer)	-	-	-	5
5(employee)	8	3	-	1
6(owner)	-	1	2	2
7(customer)	-	-	-	4
8(employee)	3	2	1	2
total	13	10	8	32

Table 3: responses to free listing task "What is a café?"

Although the answers were not subjected to a complete formal analysis, a pattern is still visible in the responses. The items were sorted under four main themes: "interior", "offered goods", "working place" and "meeting point". In both investigated cases, there is a cluster of listings relating to the theme of "meeting point", which make up more than half of the total number of items. Every informant named several items associated with this theme, which underlines the particular significance of the social function of cafés.

In "Café Rosa", the philosophy of the enterprise is not to disturb the customers in order to give them the possibility to enjoy themselves. The café is meant to be a meeting point for different types of customers and a place for their social interactions – the owners and employees explicitly remain in the background. This emphasis is also expressed by the interior, the garden and the homemade goods on offer. The free lists support my results of interviews in "Café Rosa": in the first instance, this café is a place to relax, while the type of goods offered is of lesser importance.

A comparable picture appears in "Café Viva", although under different conditions. In this case, not the place itself or a particular interior is most important, but the relations between the customers and the owners. "Café Viva" has only a limited offer, but customers are not bothered by this. They do not buy coffee "to go" – this is a place to stay for a while and to meet others. Some regular customers even come here several times a day.

Conclusions

On the first view, the differences between the two cases seem to be very obvious. "Café Rosa" has several employees, a well-designed interior, a café garden and offers a variety of homemade products. "Café Viva" is partially located in a basement, with only a limited offer and the owners have to manage all daily tasks on their own.

Bartlett and Rangelova (1997) describe two kinds of small firms in Bulgaria. The small firm as a family enterprise, privately financed with limited funds and often founded as a reaction to unemployment, is contrasted to a minor group of small enterprises with employees and a potential for economic growth. Only in the latter cases, there are sufficient resources (and willingness) for larger initial investments or to reinvest parts of the profit.

A comparison of the two cases presented here confirms this difference. The young couple who founded "Café Rosa" want to develop the enterprise and to try new business strategies. They hire employees, offer homemade quality products and advise their employees on an explicit "business philosophy". The goal of economic success is clearly visible in these strategies.

Obviously, also the owners of "Café Viva" have to earn money. The initial motivation to open the café was a reaction to unemployment, but there was no possibility to invest into the interior or to expand the range of goods offered. The owners work long hours every day without a chance of a higher turnover.

Yet another result also confirms important points made in the literature. Petrova (2010: 44ff) stresses the intertwining of private and professional life in Bulgaria. According to her observations, employees of small firms tend to see themselves as members of a "big family", and the borders between private and professional duties remain fluid.

Both cases presented here confirm this mixture of professional and private activities. There is no definite conceptual separation between free time and working time. In "Café Rosa", employees go shopping, run private errands or do small repairs of private items during working hours, in times when customer presence is low.

This overlap is visible in the other café as well, but in a different way. In "Café Viva" the relations between the owners and customers seem to be even more important than economic success. Also due to very long working hours, relations to customers form an important part of their social activities.

To summarize, for most of my informants the café is much more than a working place or a source of economic success. Founding a small firm is a potential survival strategy in times of economic crisis, but besides this, small cafés in Sofia are focal points for social relations – places to make and meet friends, and to have a good time

References

Bartlett, Will, Rangelova, Rossitsa (1997) Small Firms and Economic,Transformation in Bulgaria. In: Small Business Economics. Klewer Academic Publishers: 319 – 333.

Benovska-Sâbkova, Milena (2004) Social Networks, Coalitions, and Clientelism at Workplace in Bulgaria. In: Klaus Roth (Ed.), Arbeit im Sozialismus – Arbeit im Postsozialismus. Münster: 109-128.

— (2008) Leisure Time, Friendship Groups and Social Capital in Bulgaria. In: Klaus Roth (ed.), Sozialkapital - Vertrauen – Rechtssicherheit: postsozialistische Gesellschaften und die Europäische Union, Wien: 183-203.

Dittrich, Eckhard, Genov, Nikolaj, Kollmorgen, Raj, Oswald, Ingrid, Schrader, Heiko, Taur, Melanie, (eds.) (2006) Gesellschaftliche Transformationen, Band 2, Dittrich, Eckhard, Schrader, Heiko, Gojanov, Christo, Von Wirten und anderen Entrepreneuren, Kleinunternehmen in Bulgarien, Tchechien und der Russischen Föderation, Berlin.

Gehl, Christian (2008) Bulgarien, Schwarzmeerküste, Michael Müller Verlag, Erlangen.

Knaus, Gerald (1997) Bulgarien, Becksche Reihe, Länder, München.

Petrova, Ivanka (2010) Cultural Strategies for Mobilization in the Realm of Labour – The Socialist Realm of Labor in Bulgaria: Some Problems of the Transition to Market Economy. In: Ethnoscripts, Ethnologie Bulgariens – Bulgarische Ethnologie? 12, 1: 34 – 62.

Thiele-Dohrmann, Klaus (1997) Europäische Kaffeehauskultur, Düsseldorf, Zürich.

Doing art in Sofia: artists' livelihood strategies and the search for an "Art Scene"

Sinikka Harms

Until we started preparing for our fieldwork in 2010, Bulgaria was a "blind spot" on my mental map of Europe, as for most other participants of our research group,.. My initial interest was triggered by the euphoria Professor Kokot exuded when she first talked about Bulgaria as a country of investigation, in the seminar "Bulgaria – ethnographic overview and transformation processes" which was held in 2009/2010 at Hamburg University.

During my fieldwork, this "blind spot" became a "bright spot" in which I met artists, who were friendly and interested in what I was doing there. I often had the feeling that almost everyone I talked to was honestly surprised about the choice of doing fieldwork in Bulgaria. But they were also pleased and very helpful. Some of them became valuable informants on a regular basis; talking not only about art, but about many other topics that were important to them as well.

By doing fieldwork among artists in Sofia, I put my focus on a topic which also affects me personally. For me, painting is a way of expressing myself beyond the demands of studying or earning a living. However, I had no previous knowledge about artists or art in Bulgaria before my fieldwork. All my information on this topic was gathered during the interviews, as most of the literature and even the information on the internet was in Bulgarian and by far exceeded my grasp of this language.

In the field I used interviews, participant observation, mental maps and other ethnographic methods to gather data to answer my questions. I soon found out however, that not all methods were equally useful to get the information I needed. The major part of my data were derived from informal talks, qualitative interviews and observations of the artists´ everyday working routines.

The "Art Scene": a working concept

My initial question when starting fieldwork was: *is there an "Art Scene" in Sofia?*

To answer this question, I had to develop a working definition for the meaning of "scene" in this context. In his dissertation, Sebastian Haunss (2003) quotes different definitions of the term "*scene*", which do not necessarily refer only to art and artists, but to social and cultural "scenes" in general.

One definition can be translated as follows: "a scene emerges if people meet more and more frequently at designated places. There are enough drinks; last call orders move further into the night. The scene resembles the 18th century coffee house, the 19th century salon, the Masonic Lodge, groups and schools of the art circle, the church communities, in short, it resembles all (in)formal institutions that combine the memories of an incidence with a lifestyle that promises and cultivates continuity"[1] (Agentur Bilwet 1991: 61).

Another definition emphasizes "thematically focused cultural networks of people, who share certain material and/or mental forms of collective self-styling and who develop and stabilize similarities at specific places and times"[2] (Hitzler, Bucher, Niederbacher 2001: 20).

Based on these notions, I developed my own working concept of "Art Scene" for the purpose of my fieldwork, which refers to a specific

---

1 Quote in German original (translated by S. Harms): "Die Szene entsteht, wenn man einander immer öfter an dazu auserkorenen Orten über den Weg läuft. Es gibt genug zu trinken, die letzte Runde rückt immer mehr in die Nacht hervor. Die Szene ähnelt dem Kaffeehaus des 18. Jahrhunderts, dem Salon des 19. Jahrhunderts, der Loge, den Gruppen und Schulen der Künstlerkreise, der kirchlichen Gemeinden, kurzum all den (in)formellen Institutionen, die die Erinnerung an das Ereignis mit einem Lebensstil verbinden, in dem das Versprechen der Wiederkehr kultiviert wird."

2 Quote in German original (translated by S. Harms): "Thematisch fokussierte kulturelle Netzwerke von Personen, die bestimmte materiale und/oder mentale Formen der kollektiven Selbststilisierung teilen und Gemeinsamkeiten an typischen Orten zu typischen Zeiten interaktiv stabilisieren und weiterentwickeln."

category of people meeting at specific places on random occasions as well as on purpose. Most significantly, there must be designated locations to meet and to communicate with people who share the same values interests. These locations are not necessarily the only places to meet those people, but going there (and being seen there) signifies that one is part of this social category, or *scene*, as I call it here.

In Dona's studio (Photo: S. Harms)

The artists

Seven informants were interviewed and observed on a regular basis during my fieldwork. Three of them became very important contacts providing fundamental data. Before presenting my results in more detail, I shall first introduce the main informants. All of them agreed that I could use their real names

Dona Stoyanova (Dona), 33 years old, PhD-student and manager of the *openactstudio* (bulg. *Ve4ernact*). I met her through a woman I did yoga with while I was in Sofia. Dona became one of my main informants. We met many times for formal interviews as well as for informal talks. I visited her drawing classes on a regular basis.

Emil Chuchev (Emil), 55 years old, restorer, icon painter and manager of *Rakursi Auction House.* I met him through my informant Tsvetlana Stefanova. I did one long interview with him when I visited him at his studio house in Boyana outside of Sofia.

Ivanka Kolchakova (Vania), 30 years old, single mother, whom I "found" on the internet. We did one intensive interview at the café of the Art Academy which is located at the basement of the Academy. She is a freelance painter with no further occupation.

Svetoslav Nedev (Slav), 44 years old, freelance artist. He has no formal training as an artist. When he was 20 years old, he decided to become an artist and opened a studio of his own. He does oil paintings and from time to time digital art, like in his current project *Biotop.* When I did some internet research I came across his information but I finally met him through Vihra Barova. He became one of my main informants with whom I met several times for different interviews.

Tsvetlana Stefanova (Tsveti), 60 years old, was manager of an art gallery until a few years ago. I met with her for one interview and she accompanied me to do the interview with Emil Chuchev at Boyana.

Zefir Kukushev (Zefir), 50 years old, mural and icon painter. He studied mural painting at the National Art Academy in Sofia and then focused on icon painting. We had one interview which Vihra translated.

Zhivko Minev (Zhivko), 28 years old, PhD-student and sculptor. He has a studio with his father and brother in Mladost I. I met him through Vihra as well and met with him often. He became one of my main informants.

Dr. Vihra Barova, 29 years old, Researcher at the Bulgarian Academy of Sciences, Sofia. During the fieldwork my German research group worked together with a few PhD students, Dr. Barova and Prof. Dr. Milena Benovska. Thanks to her I was introduced to many artists.

Places for doing art

An important place for my participant observations on a regular basis was the *openactstudio (вечернакт)* run by Dona Stoyanova. At the time of my fieldwork, the studio was still located in the attic of an old industrial building in Georgi Benkovski Street, close to the city center.[3]

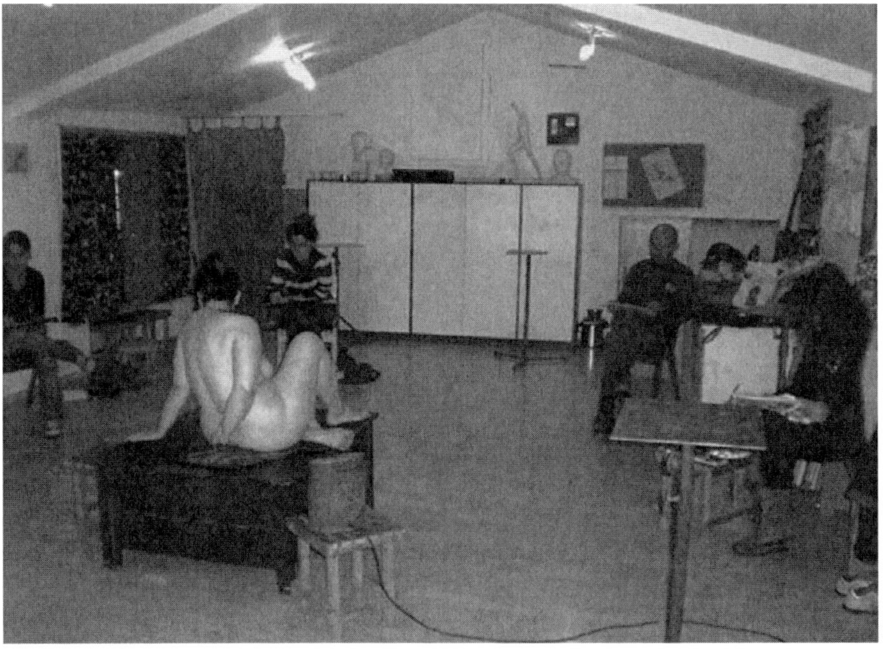

Dona's studio (Photo: S. Harms)

3 In the meantime Dona ´s studio changed location. She moved into a smaller and cheaper place.

It was a one-room studio of 40-50 square meters equipped with a huge mirror at one side of the room, drawing boards, bookshelf, clay and plaster stands and small statues Dona had made during her studies. Furthermore there was a big podium in the middle of the room, so the model could be seen from every angle and a computer which was used to play music during the drawing classes.

Another place I went to regularly is the café of the National Academy of Art called "*Café Club – Akademia*" which had been in existence for only two months at that time. Before, there had been another café in the same accommodations which had been closed for a long time.

The café is located in the basement of the Art Academy building, serving as a meeting place for students and professors. There I met with Zhivko, Dona and Vania for interviews, and I also had coffee there with Dona outside of my research. Although it is visited by many art students, I wouldn't consider it as a typical "artists' meeting place". Outside of the Academy's daily schedule, the café is hardly frequented and it is closed on the weekends. Noticeably there are no paintings, drawings or any other types of artwork on display, although the café is located in the building of the National Academy of Art.

The National Academy of Art was opened on 1 October 1896 as "The State Drawing School". In 1911 it was proposed by the staff to rename it the Academy of Art, however the name did not take effect until 1921. Presently, the National Academy of Art is considered "*to be the most prestigious Bulgarian institution for training professional artists in the field of fine and applied arts*"[4].

The open studio *Dondukov 56,* named after its street address, is a studio run by the Art Academy where students of the department for sculpture can work in a free space. Although there are four studios in the building of the Art Academy, this studio especially is for working with stone. It is located in the backyard of an old building with a big patio where one can find stones of different material and size. The patio is the

4 National Academy of Art: http://www.nha-bg.org/en/about

main working area although there are two inside spaces that belong to the studio. Working with stone means working with machines to cut the stone, to polish the stone etc. For that matter, a free space with fresh air is indispensable so that dust can disappear. My informant Zhivko Minev took care of this project when he started his doctoral program at the Art Academy in 2009. As a graduate he was dissatisfied with the possibilities students had to work on their projects in their spare time. This working space had existed before, but was not used regularly by the professors. When I went to see the studio, I could get an idea of how things work there. This is definitely a meeting place for people who do sculpture and know each other from either university or being friends. It is a space where one can relax and work at the same time, without having to follow a working schedule, or just for hanging out with people who enjoy doing the same thing, with whom one can talk and share thoughts and ideas.

When I first found the Union of Bulgarian Artists (UBA) on the internet, I expected to find a place where the Union members meet. The café *Shipka 6 (Шипка 6)*, which is in the same building as the UBA, used to be a meeting place in the past but nowadays it is nothing more than a public café. None of my informants ever spent any time of their free time at this place although Slav is a member of UBA.

The art of surviving: livelihood strategies

During my fieldwork, I quickly learned that for most of my informants, a major theme dominating their daily lives were the contradicting demands of doing art and making a living (for comparison, see Speed 2010 on artists´ livelihood strategies in Austria and Germany). Only in a very few cases, artists were able to live off of their art. A major part of this paper will therefore focus on the different ways of combining livelihood strategies with doing art in Sofia.

The following chapter describes my informants' strategies for making a living as artists in Sofia. I will focus on the economic situation of my informants in order to present the often contradicting demands of making a living while doing art, as for example a freelance artist or a student. In regards to their livelihood strategies, my informants can be divided into four categories: the freelance artists, the PhD-students, the icon and / or mural painters and the gallery manager.

Art politics/market during the communist era

During socialist times, the art market was dominated by state institutions which regularly bought art pieces and commissioned monumental works. The party obliged firms, companies, organizations and individuals to buy artwork by an exclusive group of selected artists whose loyalty to the state was beyond doubt. While the state supported the loyal artists, there were others who were not connected to the state and had to live in indigence, but remained uncompromising. They could not sell their work because in Bulgaria at that time there was no private market for independent art.

Artists, actors, authors could be found at certain bars and cafés where they gathered on a regular basis. The café *Shipka 6,* located in the same building as the UBA, is one of the locations where artists would meet back then. After the fall of socialism, a state commissioned art market no longer exists, and the weak economic situation prevents individual customers from buying art.

The example of Dona Stoyanova

One of my most important informants was Dona, a PhD-student at The National Academy of Arts in Sofia. During the time of my fieldwork, she was doing the second year of the doctoral program in sculpture and had her own studio for act drawing, *the openactstudio.* Her PhD thesis is about pre-historical sculpture considered as art from a contemporary perspective.

When I was in Sofia, the Academy was not able to pay any salaries, so Dona had to concentrate on her studio in order to pay her bills and her everyday expenses. In the meantime, she has been forced to leave this location and rent smaller rooms because she could no longer afford to keep the old studio.

Dona had started to run her own studio in 2003 in the flat of a friend, where people gathered for drawing lessons. When the flat became too small she found a new space in the gallery *Classica* which then was run by Tsveti, another informant of mine. After closing time the gallery served as Dona's studio, where people could gather and do act drawing. Every participant had to pay an entrance fee of two Leva and Tsveti received a percentage. After two years, the gallery was suspended and Dona had to find a new location for her studio. After using a spare room in a publishing house for three months, she finally found her studio in Georgi Benkovski Street which she renovated with help of her friends and a loan a friend gave her. *"It was the library of the old factory. So I thought this place has good energy"* is how she explained her choice of this attic which has no heater or bathroom.

With the help of her friends, more and more people got to know the place and it happened to be a very successful first year. After the wintertime less people came and she realized that she needed new strategies to run the studio successfully. Her aim is not to earn a lot of money, but to offer a space for a small fee to people interested in expressing their passion for the act drawing. *The openactstudio* is an open studio where everybody can go.

In order to extend her audience, the studio also offers yoga and dancing classes, philosophical lectures as well as pedagogical advanced training which are held by different teachers.

The open drawing evenings were offered from Mondays to Thursdays from 7 to 9 p.m. with a four Leva entrance fee, the drawing classes on Sundays from 1 to 7 p.m. for ten Leva per student. Workshops about working with clay and plaster for 20 Leva per person were provided as well. By renting out rooms to other teachers she can pay the rent for the studio, but she does not draw any additional income for herself.

From struggle to success: cases in comparison

As a PhD-student, Zhivko not only studies in the Art Academy, but he works in construction from time to time as well. In sharing a studio for their work, Zhivko, his father Mincho and his brother Vassil work together as sculptors. Although his father is a freelance artist as well as his brother, they also have to work in other areas to earn enough money to make a living.

After the changes in 1990, Mincho Minev had to give up his studio in the center of Sofia and rented a new studio in Studentskigrad. Because Mincho could no longer earn a family's living solely from doing sculptures, he had to take up other jobs occasionally like construction work or the restoring of old houses. Sometimes however, a request for doing a sculpture is more a matter of business than of art. Zhivko reports about feelings of humiliation in such situations, when he feels more like a salesman than like an artist. He often found himself in situations when he didn't feel passionate about working on a new sculpture, but even then customers were willing to pay a high price. In his opinion *"it is about having something expensive. [...] This is not art, it is a business. Business is something that you do and you sell it and everybody has to be pleased in a good business. In such things I am not pleased as an artist but with the money and the other one is with both. [...] It is the strategy for living*" (Interview Zhivko I, 27.09.2010). To him, it is a tragedy to work on a sculpture with all his passion which is not honored by anyone: *"the tragedy is when you make a real thing and it is not paid. From this tragedy it becomes a strategy*" (Interview Zhivko I, 27.09.2010). But even without making money, he still continues doing sculptures until now. He *"cannot live without art*" (Interview Zhivko I, 27.09.2010).

Slav also needs to take up various jobs outside his occupation as a freelance artist concentrating on oil painting. He always lived very humbly, trying to make a living from being an artist. Most of his pieces are sold to customers abroad, whereas, at least for him, there is no market in Bulgaria. Through different platforms one can find him easily on the internet[5] in Bulgaria and from abroad. He is doing exhibitions on a regular basis in order to present himself to an interested audience. His way of life reflects an uncompromising point of view, both in his art and in being a self-chosen artist, which he is not willing to sacrifice for business, money or customers. He only works at home, since he had to give up his own studio which he had for more than twenty years, three years ago due to the increasing rents.

Working at home is a strategy used by other artists as well. Vania is an oil painter who works at home in a spare room. Even though she has sold a few of her pieces, as a single mother she cannot make a living by her art alone, and needs to work outside of art as well. She studied TV-directing and worked as a cutter for several years. Since the birth of her child eighteen months ago, she tries to gain ground as an artist. Although she had some exhibitions, it is becoming increasingly difficult to afford the rents of an exhibition venue.

In contrast, Zefir is the only freelance artist with a studio of his own in the well-off district of Iztok, who can make a living by doing icon and oil painting, as well as sculptures made of stone, crystal and bronze that can be seen on his web page[6]. Most of the icons he sells to Bulgarian customers whereas his oil paintings which also remind of icons, as well as his sculptures, are mostly sold to France, USA and Germany. Not surprisingly, there is a market for icon painting among the 85% Bulgarian citizens who declare themselves as Orthodox Christians (Republic of Bulgaria, Council of Ministers, 27.09.2005)[7]. At the Art Academy he studied mural painting and in 1986 he received a certificate by the Orthodox Church that entitles him to paint icons professionally. Since after 1990 the official demand for mural painting has decreased after the political changes, he has concentrated his work on icon painting.

---

5 http://www.zeigdeinekunst.de/zdk-portal/userProfile/show/5568; http://www.artflakes.com/de/shop/nedev; http://www.kunstnet.de/Nedev

6 http://orthodox-icons.net/

7 http://www.government.bg/cgi-bin/e-cms/vis/vis.pl?s=001&p=0159&n=000003&g=

Emil graduated from the Art Academy in Sofia in 1983 and works as restorer of old paintings and frames, as well as an icon painter. As he told me, he does icon painting because he feels very connected with the special procedures and techniques of painting and gilding, and he is one of very few people in Bulgaria who still know how to do them in the original way. In his studio house in Boyana at Sofia's periphery, he employs ten people without an artistic background. Important in his work as a restorer is not the fact of having an artistic eye, value or taste, but the technical ability to for example work with different materials in order to restore paintings or frames. Here creativity is not of prime importance. Together with his son who is a painter as well, he decides what paintings to buy in order to restore them. Most of the frames that are restored by his company are property of *The National Art Gallery* and *Sofia City Art Gallery* whereas the restored paintings are going to be sold in *Rakursi-Auction house.*[8] Not only is he the owner of Rakursi-Auction house, his wife owns the contemporary art gallery *Rakursi* in the center of Sofia, and he is going to be the manager of the upcoming Gallery called *Vassilen Staykov* in which old masters will be exposed.

Is there an "Art Scene" in Sofia?

Considering the working concept of "scene" presented at the beginning of this paper, and based on the questions I asked in my interviews, I cannot come to the conclusion that there is an "Art Scene" in the sense of the term.

The (in)significance of places

Asking all informants if in their opinion there exists an "Art Scene" in Sofia, everyone answered that, at least presently, there is no such scene. Before the changes in the 1990es, the Iztok district south of the city center was considered as an artists´ neighborhood, although not as a place

8 http://www.auction-rakursi.com/en/

freely chosen by artists to live and work, but rather as a result of government regulations. Some of the artists who lived in Iztok before are still settled there, but this does not necessarily reflect a specific artistic quality of this area. More likely, they stay because they have been living there for a long time already.

When I tried to find specific places like cafés and bars where mainly artists meet, I came to the conclusion that they do not exist either, so a main indicators for the existence of a social scene, specific places to meet and communicate, does not seem to be given. Maybe the small number of my informants can be one reason for this impression, but also the results of mental mapping and free listing showed no significant results for artists meeting "*frequently at specific places*" (Agentur Bilwet 1991: 60).

In a formal sense, there is the Union of Bulgarian Artists. When I did research on the internet before starting my fieldwork, I expected this to be "the place to go", but it is rather a reminder of the old times than supporting an emerging scene. Many people stay members because they used to be in the communist times, but although the UBA has an own exhibition space in *Shipka* Street *6* and *Raiko Aleksiev*, none of my informants pointed out this place nor the Union itself as an important institution.

In front of the Alexander Nevsky Cathedral there is a regular open market area with mobile stands offering "art", crafts and (often fake) antiques mainly to a tourist audience, but according to my informants, this cannot be seen as some part of an "art scene" either. In the past however, there used to be a more genuine artists´ market in a small and very cozy garden close to the center. Every Saturday, people used to spend their free time at this place, artists as well as "non artists", but after the changes in the 1990s the garden was closed and so was the art market.

When I asked Zhivko, Dona and Slav to "draw your view of the city of Sofia" in a mental map, I expected to find places where they would go on a regular basis without pointing it out during the interview. However, only Dona drew a couple of galleries, The National Art Gallery and Sofia City Gallery. Furthermore she pictured her studio, the place where she lives and The Art Academy.

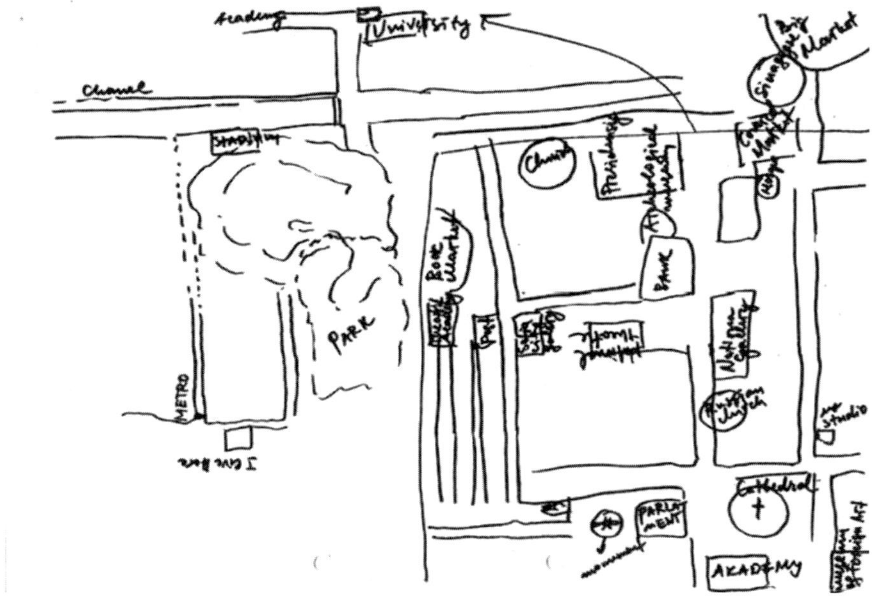

Mental Map: Dona Stoyanova

Zhivko's mental map shows his studio, the studio Dondukov 56 and his place of birth.

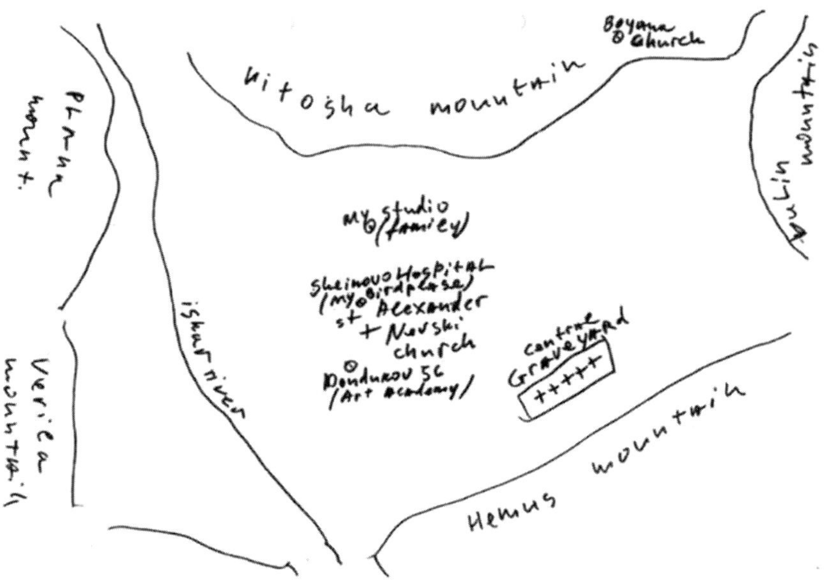

Mental Map: Zhivko Minev

When I analyzed the mental map drawn by Slav I had to realize that he did not name a single place that is in contact with art. Although he does exhibitions on a regular basis, he would not name a gallery nor mark "home" as his working space. In total, none of these mental maps reflect the fact that they were drawn by professional artists.

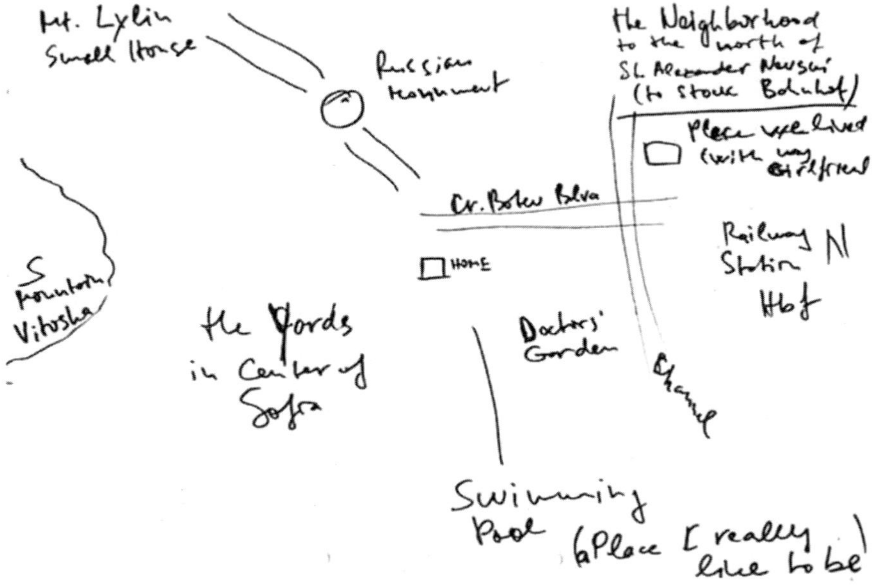

Mental Map: Svetoslav Nedev

Social relations

Another set of questions in my fieldwork refer to the connections between my informants and to the social relations they have with other artists, in order to find any connections that can be indicative for a "scene". Initially I had assumed that each of my informants was imbedded in an artistic surrounding, but I soon had to realize that this was not the case. Although each informant knows some other artists, the number was much less than expected and I could not perceive more than small individual groups of people who are interested in the same topic. Now the question may arise: at which point does a "scene" begin to be a "scene"? This may become clearer by examining individual connections between my informants, instead of concentrating on their personal networks as a whole.

The following graph shows how my informants are connected to each other, although it only shows the existence of a connection, without reference to the content and quality of their relations.

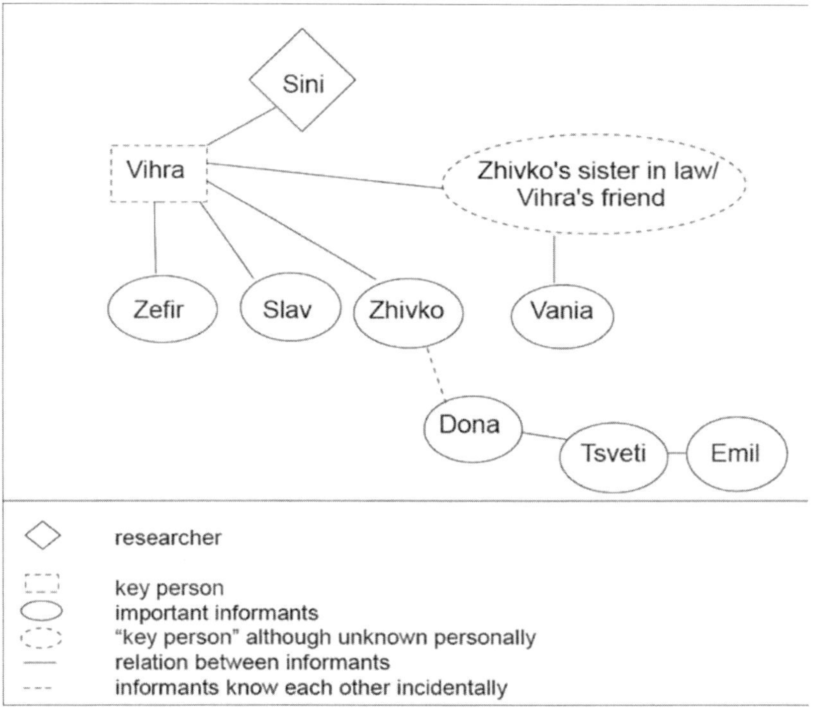

(Graphic: Sinikka Harms)

Although the graph shows a connection between individual informants, this does not mean a relation through the arts. As one can see, Vihra and her friend (who is Zhivko´s sister in law) are key nodes in the network, although I have never met Vihra´s friend. Through Vihra I got to know Slav, Zhivko and Zefir , through Vihra's friend I incidentally "found" Vania on *facebook,* an online social network community. Dona introduced me to Tsveti who introduced me to Emil. All these people know of each other, but their relations are not primarily based on their artistic activities. Some, like Dona and Zhivko, have met during their studies, but they never have been worked on joint projects nor gone to the same places in their free time in order to do art or meet other artists.

As Dona pointed out, people who participate at the drawing evenings on a regular basis could be seen as a group with a similar interest, but she would not call it a "scene". During my participant observation while I was drawing as well, I indeed noticed the same people coming regularly, but as Dona told me they came to work on their drawing abilities to apply for the academy.

Zhivko is imbedded in an artistic background by growing up with parents who are sculptors, and his siblings do arts too. Most of his friends are also doing sculptures, most of them have met during their studies. Although Zhivko has contact with a lot of people of the same profession, this still does not qualify as a "scene" as defined at the beginning of this paper. According to these definitions, a "scene" emerges when people that did not know each other before, get to know each other incidentally by frequenting specific places. These places after a while become identified with certain topics so that everybody who is interested will go there in order to meet people with a same interest, same values and so forth.

Conclusions

Through different ethnographic methods I tried to find out if there is an art scene in Sofia. Both from my own observations and from my informants' statements I derived the unanimous answer: There is *no* art scene in Sofia!

A possible explanation may be found in the political changes after 1990, when the government stopped supporting individual artists and art in general. The old state-based organizations either lost their meaning for a new generation of younger artists, or ceased to exist altogether. In consequence, many artists could no longer afford to solely concentrate on doing art. Being forced to combine different livelihood strategies, there is not much potential for creating an independent art scene. On the other hand, fewer people in Bulgaria have been able to buy and to collect art. Only slowly, Bulgarian artists are being recognized by an international art market. With growing international recognition in the future, there may also emerge an independent "art scene" in Sofia.

References

Agentur Bilwet (1991) Bewegungslehre. Botschaften aus einer autonomen Wirklichkeit. Edition ID-Archiv, Berlin, Amsterdam.

Haunss, Sebastian (2003) Identität in Bewegung. Prozesse kollektiver Identität bei den Autonomen und in der Schwulenbewegung, Wiesbaden: VS Verlag für Sozialwissenschaften, zugl. Univ. Diss. Universität Bremen.

Hitzler, Ronald; Thomas Bucher, Arne Niederbacher (2001) Leben in Szenen. Formen jugendlicher Vergemeinschaftung heute, Opladen.

Speed, Emily (2010) Artists´ livelihood strategies. a-n magazine: http://www.a-n.co.uk/publications/article/626650/626643.

Websites:

National Academy of Art: http://www.nha-bg.org/en/about

Sunny places, dark prejudices. Street musicians in Sofia

Eleonora Wewer

Back in October 2009, crossing the Dammtor Bridge in Hamburg I heard familiar tunes through the noise of roaring vehicles. Still hurrying by, I could now recognize Bulgarian folklore music in the best tradition of wedding-*chalga*[1], reminding me of my childhood days back in Sofia. I decided to take a five-minute break and just enjoy melodies and recollections. The two musicians responded to my greetings with almost virtuoso improvisations. It was a high-level performance and still, there was nearly no one there to watch it.

This reminded me of an article I had read about an experiment with Joshua Bell, a world-famous violin player who remained largely unnoticed on a cold January morning at the Washington L'Enfant Plaza Metro station despite his brilliant performance. The $32 he collected would have probably not sufficed even for a cheap ticket for his own solo performance in Boston three days earlier[2]. Was it the music or the musician, or was it the place or the ignorant audience that was to blame for a lost moment of great music? Scheduled for a field work project in Sofia, Bulgaria, I decided to search there for a possible answer.

This paper is based on field data from participant observations, informal and in-depth interviews, mental maps and network analysis,

---

1 Chalga (bulg, чалга, turk. Çalga) is a musical style characterized by "high levels of technical virtuosity coupled with rapid-fire improvisation on traditional musical motifs and scalar passages, as well as extremely fast tempos, profuse ornamentation, very loud amplified sound, and the incorporation of multiple themes, frequent key changes, and the use of complex, sometimes chromatic harmonies" (Buchanan 1996, 204). The musicians are usually referred to as "chalgadji" and the orchestras as "chalgi".

2 Weingarten, Gene. Pearls Before Breakfast. Washington Post, 8.04.2007. URL: http://www.washingtonpost.com/wp-dyn/content/article/2007/04/04/AR2007040401721.html, retrieved on 26.06.2011)

photos, video- and sound files I collected over the course of forty-days of fieldwork on the streets of Sofia, where some twenty street musicians as well as their audience talked to me about their problems, inspirations and ideas. It deals with issues like artists' social roles, their ways of coping with the ups and downs of street life and their approach toward old obstacles still staying in their way, as well as with specific strategies like implementing their skills under sometimes extreme social conditions.

In this paper, I shall first give a short historical overview of street music in Bulgaria and its present legal framework, followed by a brief sketch of key performance places in Sofia in order to distinguish them typologically in the context of the interplay between urban environment and outdoor music. Later, I shall discus street musicians' strategies to be successful as artists within a dynamic social field, present-day problems related to persisting negative social attitudes, as well as their ways to keep their artistic and social integrity nonetheless.

Current state of research

Street music, also referred to as "busking"[3], has often drawn the attention of sociologists, journalists, and ethnographers as a substantial part of public life, besides its art qualities. Prato (1984) argues that the modern-day experience of street music includes much more than the pure music. Moreover, the reception of a street performance can interact with social involvement and aesthetic experience in a specific urban environment.

3 from busk (v.) "to offer goods for sale only in bars and taprooms," 1851 (in Mayhew), perhaps from busk "to cruise as a pirate," which was used in a figurative sense by 1841, in reference to people living shiftless and peripatetic lives. The nautical term is attested since the 1660s (in a general sense of "to tack, to beat to windward"), apparently from obs. Fr. busquer "to shift, filch, prowl," which is related to It. buscare "to filch, prowl," Sp. buscar (from O.Sp. boscar), perhaps originally from bosco "wood", with a hunting notion of "beating a wood" to flush game. Online Etymology Dictionary, URL: http://www.etymonline.com/index.php?term=busker&allowed_in_frame=0,retrieved on 03.06.2011

Further developing this idea, Tannenbaum´s (1995) exploration of the New Yorker subway musicians is a rich ethnography of the local buskers' community in search of their social and cultural roots, their motivation and their economic strategies. In her view, the active exchange between the musicians on one side, and between musicians and audience on the other, contributes generally to a better quality of urban living, from the plain pleasure of listening up to the feeling of safety due to live-music in the subway areas. A small volume presenting the results of a student fieldwork project in Altona, Hamburg (Kokot et al. 2004) also focuses on performers' everyday strategies to cope with the insecure conditions of working on the streets. The potential of political action for social change through street performance is discussed by McKay (2007).

Several researchers have approached the subject from a more personal perspective. Anderberg (2011), a street performing artist herself, discusses gender problems among street artists focusing on violation and sexism towards female performers. Another focus in her work is the integration of the public space with its natural features (sceneries, acoustic, etc.) into the buskers' performance. Similarly, Ferrell (2001) focuses on the changes that particular occupants of the street, like buskers, squatters, beggars, etc. can force onto the public space by influencing or resisting urban policy and legal control, as according to the author, "*to move through space is to remake it*" (Ferrell 2001: 69).

Researchers in Bulgaria, too, are slowly discovering street music as a cultural category, although so far, there have been only two domestic studies on the topic: Mariela Hristova's small book (1997) on street musicians in the 1980^s and 1990^s is an ethnography of Bulgarian street music of the first post-socialist decade. With regards to methodology however, the monograph remains in the tradition of socialist musicology, thus offering little cross-cultural reflections. Ivan Dimitrov's article (2010) can be taken as a first attempt to descriptively cover the buskers' scene in Sofia and to discuss their place in urban culture. Still, much more remains to be explored about the local musicians within a global context.

History of Bulgarian street music until 1989

Contemporary street music in Bulgaria derives from two different traditions. At the end of the 19th century, a new type of urban musical practice appeared: the so-called *chalgi* (orchestra), usually consisting of two to eight members with a poly-functional repertoire of folklore and popular melodies, mostly to be heard at weddings, theatre performances and public shows (Vulchinova-Chendova 2000:43). Simultaneously, a new category of mobile entertainers emerged – the so-called funfair musicians (*панаирджийски музиканти*), who were criss-crossing the country between 1878 and 1940 joining ambulant salesmen on their way through fun- and trade fairs. A certificate issued after auditions before a special commission in Sofia, allowed successful applicants to call themselves "public folklore bards" (площаден народен певец) (State Archive, Abstract No 247, Fund 143, Op. 8, cited in Hristova 1997, 12). Besides music, their performances could include theatre, storytelling and satire in the tradition of medieval street-performances[4].

During the socialist period, street musicians experienced increasing pressures of administrative control. The attestations of musical quality, which had been applied up to 1950^s, were then replaced by ideological ones. In 1951 a circular letter by the State Committee of Science, Art and Culture declared new guidelines for socialist outdoor music, whose repertoire was with immediate effect to include Bulgarian folklore and contemporary socialist music, as well as Russian and Soviet songs (ibid.).

Six years later a complete banishment followed, based on the State Act 258 of 1958 "*On resolving some key issues with the gypsy population in PR Bulgaria*" (За уреждане въпросите на циганското население в НР България). Aimed originally at the Roma ethnic group, by prohibiting all forms of "nomadic life and beggary" the whole range of ambulant trades such as mobile sales- and craftsmen, fortunetellers,

4 "They satirized political and religious opponents, preached crusaders, sang funeral laments upon the death of famous patrons, and the support of their poetical powers was often in demand by princes and nobles" (Chaytor 1912, 31).

healers, and street musicians was criminalized simultaneously. Infringements were to be punished with the whole vigor of the new socialist laws – fines up to 1000 BGN, penal servitude, or imprisonment up to five years. Violators were subjected to public defamation with the active help of institutions like party activist groups, local militiamen or social service worker organizations. It is remarkable that an explicit mentioning of street music was nowhere to be found. Hristova (1997: 14) concludes that they were included by default, as some of them were Roma who occupationally maintained a nomadic way of life.

Street music as an administrative category

According to the information I had previously gathered about the legal framework, street musicians are obliged to apply to the municipal office public order which issues licenses for places and playing times. For my fieldwork, I had planned to conduct an expert interview with a representative of the city administration about legal and administrative issues regarding street music. Regrettably however, my attempts to get in touch with a person in charge proved unsuccessful, since there this position is (still) not occupied despite being required by law. Nevertheless, when visiting the municipality some friendly ladies from the administration introduced me to the simple procedure of applying for a license as a street musician in Sofia. Since 50 years, there are no more state exams (s. above); the licenses are issued free of charge for a period of six months by the municipal administration. Candidates submit a free-form application where they list the desired performance places as well as the playing times. Furthermore they agree to comply with public regulations and to refrain from performances during the rest times. Their earnings are still tax-free.

All of my interview partners were in possession of such a license. Although "no authority checks on it" (male, 61, 28.09.2010) it is an important proof of legitimacy which can be shown anytime and which may also serve as a "reservation ticket" for the performance spot, in case of conflicts with competing musicians.

There is also no limit to the duration of performances. All of my informants were free to decide where, how often and how long they would play according to their own financial needs for the day, the crowd's attention, collegial ethic or their own pleasure[5].

Choosing the right corner - Sofia as urban field and place of street music

Sofia is a very vivid southern-type city, the noise from constantly speeding cars mixing with music tunes streaming out of every café. The local buskers fit in this loud soundscape by performing in public locations which are highly frequented during the day, thus adapting themselves to the dynamic streams of passing citizens and tourists.

Consequently, Sofia's downtown area is the centre of street music, stretching between Eagle Bridge (Орлов Мост) and Boris' Garden (Борисовата градина) to the Southeast and Pirotska street to the Northwest, and between Lion Bridge (Лъвов Мост) at the North and South Park (Южен Парк) at the South. The area includes some of the most favoured places in the city, e.g. the Central Department Store (*ЦУМ*), the University St. Kliment Ohridski, the National Theatre, the National Palace of Culture (*НДК*), as well as some of the biggest shopping promenades and four central parks in Sofia.

In addition, some interviewees provided me with information about musical practices beyond these locations. Certain sites of family celebrations such as maternity clinics and registrar´s offices, were of particular interest for the street musicians. Following a tradition for newly wedded couples or newly born babies and their families to receive

5 I had informers playing spontaneously (male, 19) as well as playing with hard discipline (female, 49, male, 68). One would play until her daily need was covered, the blind-man band of five played exactly two hours and went home, "to give their hearts some rest" (male, 52, 20.09.2010).

musical greetings right off the happy event, *chalgi*-bands and soloists take up such opportunities with much enthusiasm, thus turning distant and lesser frequented places into street performance spots. Unfortunately, I received this information much too late to be able to explore it in detail, but the phenomenon could definitely be interesting for a follow-up study.

Places of listening - a typology of locations

A great deal of Sofia´s street music is performed at spaces and places of transition – at bus stops, subway underpasses or on big shopping streets. Vitosha Boulevard, by far the most expensive shopping area in Sofia, is a good example in this regard, particularly the 1,2 km long section between *ZUM* and *NDK* which has been converted into a pedestrian area. The street is dominated by its many luxurious fashion stores, intermingling with small business, residential buildings and many leisure establishments – cafés, restaurants, bingo-halls, etc., all of them targeting on affluent clientele. Cast-iron benches are installed on the broad sidewalks and form small verdant recreational areas. This colourful mixture of commerce, work and leisure makes Vitosha a popular meeting point in Sofia, where locals and tourists form a potential audience for a large number of street musicians (I observed up to twenty different performances at the same time).

The buskers perform on the sidewalks between pedestrians or in front of shops and house entrances, which often leads to conflicts with the residents. The constant drifts of passers-by narrow the already small performing spots, some musicians literally being tripped over. For that reason, most musicians change locations frequently in search of better positions, delivering short performances as long as no one complains.

Vitosha Boulevard is an example for what Schafer calls "places of unfocused listening" (Schafer 1984, cit. in Dimitrov 2010, 2) which represent a common modus operandi of buskers in Sofia. In such an environment, it is likely for the performer to remain completely anonymous and they are not heard very clearly. Although professionals may see this situation as jeopardizing their reputation, some amateurs use it as a chance to make small profit even with a poor performance. "*Here you can make mistakes and no one would even notice, because of the noise*", remarked a respondent (male, 54. 7.09.2010) playing his e-piano at the intersection of Orlov Most, one of the busiest traffic locations in Sofia. Prato argues that such informal music practices "tend to mix with the environment, to be part of it and to be perceived in distraction" (Prato 1984, 152). The physical presence of a musician playing for some change is more important than the quality of the music played in such noise-filled locations.

In contrast to these spaces of transition, Sofia´s numerous parks and gardens which were explicitly designed as places of relaxation, offer an environment favorable to more concentrated, or at least less unfocused, listening. The Singing Fountains Square in front of the National Theatre is such a place. It is located between the National Theatre, the National Bank and the National Art Gallery. A broad cobblestone square separates it from the theatre building, old trees spread shadows over alleys, playgrounds and outdoor cafés where once Georgi Dimitrovs Mausoleum[6] stood.

There are no shops there except for one music store. The theatre building forms the optical centre of the park, the freshly painted façade is imposingly illuminated by night. The park has always been associated with the Arts, with numerous galleries and theatres in the immediate proximity. The area is often used for art performances or fashion shows. At the time of my field work, there was an open-air photo exhibition followed by a puppet theatre festival.

Under an old tree on the north corner aside from the fountain, a Roma trio (three men playing trumpet, accordion and drums) has been

6 Georgi Dimitrov (1882 - 1949) was the first Socialist Prime Minister of Bulgaria (1946 till 1949). After his death the embalmed body was put on public honor in a specially built Mausoleum. In 1990, following a State Act on the matter, Dimitrov's remains were buried in the Sofia Central Cemetery and the mausoleum building was blown up.

entertaining their numerous listeners with salon music, jazz and pop for ten years now on a regular basis, representing a sedentary type of buskers′ strategies.

These are the places to watch professional performances directly involving the audience. I saw an elderly couple dancing cha-cha and tango to the sound of the Roma trio. Deep silence prevailed over the University Garden as a string-quartet played Vivaldi. Usually however, the buskers do not stay in focus of attention; but are perceived as a part of the urban landscape. It takes specific competences to win over the non-focused listening, such as a sharp vision of the social dynamic, flexible spatial orientation, the ability to communicate with the audience and last but not least, strong nerves.

Playing in the streets: strategies and necessities

"To play on a hat" (свиря на шапка) can be seen as a strategy of urban subsistence (Kokot 2006, 2). There is a fair chance not to come away empty-handed, but none of my informants would see the street as a stable source of profit. Still, the street offers the chance to reach a potential audience or even an employer, and to so attain more solid sources of income. This is for instance the case with a band called "Oratniza" (www.oratniza.com), whose members after a year of outdoor playing got their first major contract with a high-class Sofia music club. They still occasionally play on the street, not just for fun, but also for self-promotion.

Equipment

Being a busker in Sofia takes more than just the "three guitar accords and a slightly harsh voice", as claimed in a popular Bulgarian song[7]. Playing

7 Georgi Minchev „Blessed Years (The Rock'n'roll was young)" (Блажени години рокендролът беше млад). To be seen on http://www.youtube.com/watch?v=p_sNnbvlZ_4 (retrieved on 1.10.2011)

on the street also requires specific knowledge about invisible frontiers, obstacles, risks, and discomforts.

Sine qua non is the suitable equipment, which ought to be light and compact, as it is usually set up and dismantled several times a day. As it has to be carried through the city, its volume should not exceed the usual size of hand luggage, as otherwise the artists who mostly use public transport, would have to pay an extra fee.

In consequence, a busker's inventory in Sofia contains at least one musical instrument (and its case), a bottle of water (or other drinks), a folding chair (which can be cleared off right away in case of danger), scores and a music stand, occasionally their own CDs for sale, an official license and a collecting box. This standard package is often enhanced by (mostly household) items functionally converted to make outdoor work easier, such as multicolored clothespins to fix the scores to the stand, big synthetic-fibre shopping bags (which Bulgarians mockingly call "Bulberrys") sometimes replacing the cases and hiding the instruments if needed, or laundry lines and skipping ropes to fix the collecting box to the instruments or to the busker's foot for theft protection.

The collecting box (photo: E. Wewer)

Most street musicians I saw in Sofia still place different head coverings in front of their stands to collect money. Less traditional, but possibly more convenient, the same purpose may be served by instrument cases or different household items such as coffee- or detergent tins, beer cans or simple cardboard boxes. These items often bear special sentimental value for their owners – a plastic box once was a jewellery chest of the deceased wife, a scruffy old beer can reminded one of my respondents of the first beer he earned by playing on the street. From a functional point of view, all collecting boxes offer a fast and secure way to collect the takes. Every handsome sum was immediately put safe, and the quickness of clearing them away pointed to a long-practiced routine.

Repertoires and the pressure to adapt

Street musicians in Sofia offer a rich repertoire including folklore music with or without jazz elements, European classical music as well as popular local composers, evergreens, rock & pop, R&B, country and lots of musical hybrids. With the exception of *chalga*, which literally blasts out of every second café or car anyway, there is no music style left unattended and especially on warm sunny days, a wide range of musical tastes can be satisfied.

In my field work, I did not meet any musical "all-rounder", which confirmed my initial assumption that the musicians determine their style before deciding to play outdoors, and remain mostly true to it. However, if the opportunity arises, within their style they are always ready for improvisations. As the following example shows, flexibility of repertoire is a core element of a specific approach which I would define as a "chameleon" strategy.

Victory Day [September 9] used to be forcefully celebrated during the socialism with nationwide manifestations. In 2010, the street musicians in Sofia reacted to this date either seriously or ironically, depending on their individual political preferences. On this day, the e-piano performer at Orlov Most had decorated his keyboard with red carnations while he was listlessly playing some resistance-songs of the 1940s. Similar samples sneaked through the evergreens of the Roma trio, flavoured with the snappy comments of their soloist of the occasion, all this to much amusement of the onlookers.

Essential to this strategy is the ability to detect the tastes of the audience and to respond adequately, according to time and situation. In support of this assumption, I observed examples of shifting the repertoire on the sight of "special visitors" – generous tourists, good looking women, or children. A member of the Roma-trio blew trumpet kisses every time a handsome woman passed by. The same musicians shifted straight off to emblematic national tunes once they had detected the nationality of a passing tourist group. Such practical wisdom takes sometimes years, sometimes just a helping hand (a.k.a. a friendly tourist guide who quickly reveals the nationality) to acquire.

The Roma Trio (photo: E. Wewer)

Social (self)-organisation

Taking into account the difference between bands and soloists, social relations among street musicians seem rather loose and unstructured.

My questions about social relations based on emotional, financial or institutional help, showed that most of my informants only sporadically make use of their contacts among fellow musicians. If at all, such contacts are used for the sole purpose of financial support, while instrumental (in terms of borrowing musical instruments) or emotional help is rarely asked for.

Successfully functioning networks do exist among some groups of professionally trained musicians, where personal and professional levels interweave, such as the blind musicians′ band "The Merry Boys" who have been together for a decade, or a string quartet formed by four fellow students of the Musical Academy. The majority of street musicians in Sofia however operate as "lone fighters" who seldom keep in touch with their colleagues. Most solo performers even do not want such contacts. They see themselves as unique and independent individuals and want to remain so, be it because of their specific performances or for fear of having to split up the revenues.

Among predominantly younger musicians, social networks sometimes materialize in spontaneous one-time alliances for a gig, but they usually fall apart again soon afterwards. Most of my informants see neither opportunity nor necessity to set up institutionalised forms of organization. Firstly, this may be due to frustrating experiences with the socialist enforcement of obligatory membership. Secondly, this manifest individualism might be a strategy to remain inconspicuous *vis-a-vis* state authorities or potential taxes.

Values in transition: "We are no beggars"

Apart of the show element, the social prestige of street musicians is everything but positive. Most of my respondents, regardless of their age or gender, reported on being discredited as "hookers" (female respondents) or "beggars" (both female and male respondents). A lack of social acceptance was mentioned as a problem in most of my interviews. It dazzled me that even older (over 40) female musicians felt obliged to fiercely deny accusations of being concealed prostitutes, defending street music as a legitimate way to earn money. Complex historical and social interdependencies contribute to the still negative image of street performers in Bulgaria.

One reason may lie in the potential competition for urban public space between groups of uncertain reputation. On the urban stage, the street musicians are by far not the only players. A colorful mixture of food- and newspaper vendors, fortunetellers, beggars, or political activists bears them company, some acting autonomously, others interacting with the buskers and occasionally serving them as impresarios, bodyguards or interlocutors. This coexistence can be profitable as well as damaging. During my observations in September 2010 I saw places being taken over by beggars, shortly after the street musicians had gone. I witnessed, too, how buskers, voluntarily or not, shared the same spaces with Roma fortune-tellers within a distance of two to three metres. On one occasion, a blind singer, who apparently got angry at his miserable profit as a musician, just grabbed his white stick and started begging literally in the shift of seconds, which may have made it difficult for his potential audience to place him back again among the artists later.

Another element of the negative social image lies in the nature of the commodity "street music". Being performed outdoors and without an entrance fee, street music lacks a price tag. Sometimes this free accessibility brings real economic benefits, like surprisingly generous donations within the range of hundreds of Euros (female, 49, 16.09.2010) although these remain rare exceptions. Still, the absence of clearly defined prices and the unrestricted access may lead to an equation between buskers and beggars, who both depend on the generosity of passers-by.

Earlier in this paper, I already mentioned the precarious conditions for street musicians under the notorious State Act 258. The fact that many artists were descendants of stigmatized ethnic groups, even worsened official restrictions against mobile professions and fostered their further social decline. This low social acceptance persists up to the present, even if the ethnicity component has changed significantly since then.

In contrast to Hristova (1997), I argue that this is not a typical Bulgarian phenomenon. In a historical perspective this is rather an old topic which has been explored amongst others by Danckert (1963) as well as by Küther (1983) within the concept of "infamous occupations".

Since the European middle ages, certain occupations, travelling performers, religious or ethnic minorities were stigmatized as vagrants. They were denied access to craftsmen' guilds and excluded from inheritance laws. In many cases a mobile form of existence was the reason for stigmatization, or they were practically forced to roam around in the search of temporary employment. In basically sedentary, strongly stratified societies, these groups were perceived as disturbing elements without a fixed place of their own, and as a potential threat to the natural order. On the other hand, some of these occupations were associated with supernatural forces, "bound to primal secrets of life and death" (Danckert 1963:17, transl. EW).

Similar attitudes can be found in the present social (non)-acceptance of street musicians in Sofia, who are still associated with the image of a "rootless tree" (durvo bez koren) (female 25, 22.09.2010). Half of my informants live under precarious financial conditions around the poverty threshold[8]. Many of them have no settled family (<20 %) and the majority (87%) work in various occasional jobs of low esteem such as e.g. junk-dealers, which in turn adds fuel to the already present social disapproval. In this context, one of my key informants´ endeavour to earn a B.A. degree at the University of Sofia (she started her studies at the age of 49) can be seen as an attempt to disavow the "prostitute" image and to raise her social status.

Although the experience of stigmatization was an important topic among all my informants regardless of gender or age, there is a clear cut between the generations regarding approaches and strategies to handle it. The first generation (today between 40-60) of post-socialist buskers take on the burden of the past with more or less dignity, defending themselves with the argument that street music is a normal job worth recognition. Their young followers of the second generation, today between 18 and 35, go even further in their artistic self-perception. Just merely influenced by attitudes of the past, they take their talents as an asset, see themselves as enrichment to the urban space:

8 According to the National Statistical Institute the poverty line for 2009 amounts to BGN 185. URL: http:// http://www.nsi.bg/otrasal.php?otr=21&a1=2381&#cont (retrieved on 12.09.2001)

> "There should be at least ten times more buskers than there are now, so that people feel better. If on every street there were a couple of musicians there would be music there, not the horrid screeching of the cars, so you would walk on a completely different street. Your attention would be focusing on the real vibration, the one of the music. Thus people grow up, they can let go of things they don't need and the common sense will grow better and live in a better reality." (male, 19, 15.09.2010).

Conclusions

Since 1989, many street musicians play in the urban public space of Sofia, mainly for economic reasons, but also to have fun, to entertain or even to become a star. A strategy of prime importance is the choice of a suitable place, so knowledge of the best sites throughout the city is a crucial condition for success. Acquiring this knowledge is not difficult in a town like Sofia – it takes a couple of days walking and good friends to point you into the right direction. An active lively contact with the audience and a proficiency to follow the crowd's tastes are further assets ensuring economic success.

The street musicians must constantly adapt to the dynamic social field in which they are performing. According to their mobility, there are two main types in Sofia: the nomadic ones wandering through the city in search of best places, while others establish themselves in a particular location and try to appropriate it with time. If successful, this is a way to enjoy a core audience and better profit.

Economical marginal and socially stigmatised on the streets of Sofia, the image of street musicians still is predominantly associated with discredited activities: "Working on the street" is strongly linked to the semantics of underpaid, hard labour, instability and disrespect. Single female performers are particularly affected by persisting negative attitudes to "women of the street". This is still notably strong among elderly citizens who often openly insult and humiliate them. Complex cultural motives lie behind this stigmatization: on one side, social attitudes much older than the performers manifest themselves on a daily basis. On the other side, the persisting individualism among the musicians weakens their social and institutional presence and does not help to improve their poor acceptance. Furthermore, the nature of the public space makes it difficult for both performers and audience to sink into the atmosphere of a concentrated listening, which turns the music into a part of the urban landscape with little chance to savour it. Within the ongoing trend to "reclaim the streets" however, there may be a fair chance for street music to upgrade its prestige.

References

Anderberg, Kirsten (2011) 21st Century Essays on Street Performing (or Busking). Ventura. [Kindle Edition].

Buchanan, Donna (1996) Wedding Musicians, Political Transition, and National Consciousness in Bulgaria. In: Slobin, Mark (ed.). Retuning Culture: Musical Changes in Central and Eastern Europe. Durham [et al.]: Duke University Press, pp. 200-230.

Chaytor, Henry John (1912) The Troubadours. Cambridge: Cambridge University Press. (http://www.fullbooks.com/The-Troubadours1.html. Retrieved 12.07.2011).

Danckert, Werner (1963): Unehrliche Leute: die verfemten Berufe. Bern [et al.]: Francke.

Dimitrov, Ivan (2010) Ulicnite muzikanti v Sofia [Street musicians in Sofia]. In: Seminar_BG. Online spisanie za kulturni izsledvanija. 2/2010 (http://www.seminar-bg.eu/index2.php?option=com_content&do_pdf=1&id=247, retrieved on 21.02.2011).

Ferrell, Jeff (2001) Tearing Down the Streets. Adventures in Urban Anarchy. New York [et al.]: Palgrave for St. Martin's Press.

Hristova, Mariela (1997) Ulicnite muzikanti ot kraja na 80-te i 90-te godini na XX vek. Sofia.

Kokot, Waltraud et al. (2004) „Die härteste Bühne der Welt…“: Straßenmusik in Hamburg; ethnologische und musikwissenschaftliche Annäherungen. Hamburg.

Kokot, Waltraud, Astrid Wonneberger (2006) Urbane Subsistenz. In: Ethnoscripts 4/2006, Jg. 8. S. 2-6. Hamburg.

Küther, Carsten (1983) Menschen auf der Straße. Vagierende Unterschichten in Bayern, Franken und Schwaben in der zweiten Hälfte des 18. Jahrhunderts. Göttingen.

McKay, George (2007) ‘A soundtrack to the insurrection‘: street music, marching bands and popular protest. Parallax vol. 13: 1, pp. 20-31. http://salford.academia.edu/georgemckay/Papers/117976/A_soundtrack_to_the_insurrection_street_music_marching_bands_and_popular_protest Retrieved on 20.07.2011.

Prato, Paolo (1984) Music in the streets: the example of Washington Square Park in New York City. Popular Music, 4, pp 151-163.

Tannenbaum, Susie J. (1995) Underground Harmonies. Music and Politics in the Subways of New York. Ithaca, New York: Cornell University Press.

Vulchinova-Chendova, Elissaveta (2000) Gradskata tradizionna instrumentalna praktika i orkestrovata kultura v Bulgaria – sredata na XIX – kraja na XX vek. Sofia.

Weingarten, Gene (2007) Pearls Before Breakfast. Washington Post, 8.04.2007. URL: http://www.washingtonpost.com/wp-dyn/content/article/2007/04/04/AR2007040401721.html, retrieved on 26.06.2011)

lines

Beiträge zur Stadtforschung aus dem Institut für Ethnologie der Universität Hamburg

hrsg. von Prof. Dr. Waltraud Kokot

Waltraud Kokot (Ed.)

Beyond the White Tower - Transformations in Thessaloniki

Ethnographic case studies on local aspects of urban change

To most visitors passing through the city on their way to the beaches of Chalkidiki or to the Greek Islands, Thessaloniki means little more than its most famous tourist sites: the White Tower and the adjacent waterfront, the fortress dominating the upper city, and a few monuments from ancient, Byzantine or Ottoman times. But such reduced impressions do little justice to the rich multicultural past of the city, nor to its present position as a cultural and economic centre of northern Greece and a gate to the Balkans.

Bd. 4, 2008, 136 S., 19,90 €, br., ISBN 978-3-8258-0917-1

Astrid Wonneberger (Ed.)

Cultural Contrasts in Dublin

A montage of ethnographic studies

Up to the 1990s, Dublin and Irish urban cultures had only been marginally studied by cultural and social anthropologists, even though the Greater Dublin Area has been home to almost one third of the Republic's population for several decades. From this time anthropologists slowly became aware of the variety of cultural groups and topics which shape Ireland's capital.

This growing awareness went hand in hand with the major economic, architectural, social and cultural changes which Dublin was experiencing. Sparked by Ireland's membership of the EU (then EEC) and accelerated by the Celtic Tiger economy and increasing numbers of immigrants, the city has turned into a multicultural space of a variety unprecedented before.

The articles in this book are based on a student research project in Dublin in 2006, presenting four ethnographic case studies ranging from immigration and the formation of new religious groups to survival strategies of the urban homeless.

Bd. 6, 2011, 144 S., 19,90 €, br., ISBN 978-3-643-90159-0

LIT Verlag Berlin – Münster – Wien – Zürich – London

Auslieferung Deutschland / Österreich / Schweiz: siehe Impressumsseite